Turning Psychology
Contextual Analysis

This groundbreaking book shows how we can build a better understanding of people by merging psychology with the social sciences. It is part of a trilogy that offers a new way of doing psychology focusing on people's social and societal environments as determining their behaviour, rather than internal and individualistic attributions.

Putting the 'social' properly back into psychology, Bernard Guerin turns psychology inside out to offer a more integrated way of thinking about and researching people. Going back 60 years of psychology's history to the 'cognitive revolution', Guerin argues that psychology made a mistake, and demonstrates in fascinating new ways how to instead fully contextualize the topics of psychology and merge with the social sciences. Covering perception, emotion, language, thinking, and social behaviour, the book seeks to guide readers to observe how behaviours are shaped by their social, cultural, economic, patriarchal, colonized, historical, and other contexts. Our brain, neurophysiology, and body are still involved as important interfaces, but human actions do not originate inside of people so we will never find the answers in our neurophysiology. Replacing the internal origins of behaviour with external social contextual analyses, the book even argues that thinking is not done by you 'in your head' but arises from our external social, cultural, and discursive worlds.

Offering a refreshing new approach to better understand how humans operate in their social, cultural, economic, discursive, and societal worlds, rather than inside their heads, and how we might have to rethink our approaches to neuropsychology as well, this is fascinating reading for students in psychology and the social sciences.

Bernard Guerin has worked in both Australia and New Zealand researching and teaching to merge psychology with the social sciences. His main research now focuses on contextualizing 'mental health' behaviours, working with Indigenous communities, and exploring social contextual analyses especially for language use and thinking.

Exploring the environmental and social foundations of human behaviour
Series editor
Bernard Guerin
Professor of Psychology, University of South Australia

Can you imagine that everything people do, say, and think is shaped directly by engaging with our many environmental and social contexts? Humans would then really be part of their environment.

For current psychology, however, people only engage with metaphorical 'internal' environments or brain events, and everything we do somehow originates hidden in there. But what if all that we do and think originated out in our worlds, and what we call 'internal' is merely language and conversations that were also shaped by engaging in our external discursive, cultural, and societal environments?

Exploring the Environmental and Social Foundations of Human Behaviour is an exciting new book series about developing the next generation of ways to understand what people do, say, and think. Human behaviour is shaped through directly engaging in our diverse contexts of resources, social relationships, economics, culture, discourses, colonization, patriarchy, society, and the opportunities afforded by our birth contexts. Even language and thinking arise from our external social and discursive contexts, and so the 'internal' and brain metaphors will disappear as psychology becomes merged with the social sciences.

The series is therefore a-disciplinary and presents analyses or contextually engaged research on topics that describe or demonstrate how human behaviour arises from direct engagement with the worlds in which we are embedded.

In this series:

Turning Psychology into Social Contextual Analysis

Bernard Guerin

Routledge
Taylor & Francis Group

LONDON AND NEW YORK

First published 2021
by Routledge
2 Park Square, Milton Park, Abingdon, Oxon OX14 4RN

and by Routledge
52 Vanderbilt Avenue, New York, NY 10017

Routledge is an imprint of the Taylor & Francis Group, an informa business

© 2021 Bernard Guerin

The right of Bernard Guerin to be identified as author of this work has been asserted by him in accordance with sections 77 and 78 of the Copyright, Designs and Patents Act 1988.

British Library Cataloguing-in-Publication Data
A catalogue record for this book is available from the British Library

Library of Congress Cataloging-in-Publication Data
A catalog record has been requested for this book

ISBN: 978-0-367-89810-6 (hbk)
ISBN: 978-0-367-89811-3 (pbk)
ISBN: 978-1-003-02126-1 (ebk)

Typeset in Times
by Newgen Publishing UK

Contents

Figures

Tables

Preface

As I hope the reader will discover, this series of books is not about providing a new theory of psychology, and especially not a 'grand theory', even though the contents might suggest that. It is also not providing a new philosophy, except in a broad sense not related to Western philosophy.

The approach argues, in fact, that words do not have 'meaning' nor do they represent, refer to, or express anything and that argues against the whole Western tradition of philosophy. The only thing words do is to change the behaviour of other people *given the right social contexts*. And that is all this huge collection of words is trying to do.

Most of my words that follow are therefore trying to get you, the reader, to observe the world in new ways; be sensitized to see things you did not see before, and then act in new ways on that basis where appropriate. Most of current psychology, I argue, is just looking in the wrong places for answers and explanations. Because they do not find the answers there, they invent even more abstract words and use correlations to support them, so it looks as if we have discovered something.

The first book in this new trilogy goes back to before the 'cognitive revolution' and shows that the whole reasoning for even having a revolution was mistaken. Psychology took a wrong turn by the assumption that humans must 'go beyond the information given'. Instead, I show how all the subsequent ideas of 'processing information' and 'internal constructions and representations' were really about the social uses of language, and all these ideas and theories can be replaced when we 'turn psychology inside out'. Language use is shown to be externally driven by properly observing all social and societal contexts and realizing that thinking is just language use not said out loud. I then show how we can replace our 'psychology' with the diverse life contexts in which we are immersed, and explore how we can contextualize perception, emotion, and thinking in this way so they do not originate 'inside our heads'.

The second book in this new trilogy shows how the other social sciences have already explored our life contexts, and once we are rid of the current abstract explanations in terms of an 'internal' world, we can merge 'psychology' into the social sciences to form a rich analysis of how humans adapt and become attuned to all of our life contexts. In particular, I explore how our behaviours are now hugely shaped by the modern worlds of capitalism, neoliberalism, and bureaucracy, and how the Marxist frameworks are incompatible with current psychology but can be merged in a contextual approach. Several of the very 'individualistic' ideas embedded in current psychology are then shown to arise directly from our complex social, cultural, and societal worlds, and not from 'inside' us. In particular, I turn the 'psychology' of beliefs, the self, the arts, religious behaviours, and many of the 'individual' phenomena of social psychology inside out, to show their external contexts of origin.

The third book in this new trilogy applies social contextual analysis to the important area of 'mental health'. The behaviours observed in 'mental health' issues are treated here as ordinary behaviours that have been shaped in very bad life situations to become exaggerated and trapped because alternative solutions are blocked. To support the many current attempts to stop using the *Diagnostic and Statistical Manual of Mental Disorders* (DSM), I explore all the individual DSM-listed behaviours and show how they can be shaped by living in bad situations with no alternatives, and are not the result of any brain 'disorders'. The types of bad life situations are explored further, and it is shown that many other behaviours are shaped in addition to the 'mental health' behaviours: violence, bullying, escape, alternative lifestyles, self-harm, exploitation of other people, crime, drug taking. It is suggested that all those people involved in any of these outcomes from bad life situations, professionals, and first-hand experiencers, should pool their expertise and integrate how we can *fix the bad life situations rather than try and fix the person*. Based on these conclusions, interventions for fixing bad life situations are explored, including fixing local issues, fixing those bad social situations that interfere with language use and thinking, and how we might begin to tackle those bad situations produced by our current societal contexts and that are leading to new 'mental health' behaviours: capitalism, neoliberalism, bureaucracy, stratifications, colonization, and patriarchy.

Acknowledgements

The books in this series are a culmination of over 45 years of thinking and researching about these issues, taking every approach seriously, and learning from all of psychology and the social sciences (especially sociology, social anthropology, and sociolinguistics). There are too many people to thank (or even remember) from whom I have learned, so I want to really thank again everyone I have acknowledged in my previous books. You know who you are, I hope. All my students from all my courses have also helped shape my writing when I have used them to try out new ideas and analyses—many thanks.

I also want to thank the staff at Routledge for their belief in this trilogy (and the previous one) and their excellent editing and production work.

A note on referencing

First, each book of the series of six is self-contained, and I have aimed to make them readable alone. However, for those brave souls attempting to see the bigger picture, I use cross-referencing of volume number and chapter in this way: V5.7 refers to Chapter 7 of Volume 5 in the series.

Second, I wish to say upfront that this book comes from reading the work of many researchers and authors across all of psychology and all of the social sciences over many years. In my earlier books I have given hundreds of references to the work of others that has shaped my thinking, even when I disagree. However, I know that referencing slows down a lot of readers whom I would like to take something away from these books that might be of use to them. Many of my intended readers also do not have the privilege of being able to track down the references in any case.

For these reasons, I am being a very bad academic in these books and mostly refer to my own summary works. This current book has been intentionally written so that it can be understood without knowing those earlier books, but to academics (real ones, not me) this causes distress because it looks like I am claiming others' ideas when I use a lot of self-referencing. I certainly do not intend this but having thousands of references interrupting the text causes distress to other readers. This time, I am balancing the distress the other way. You can find the references in my earlier books if needed.

Obviously, where I use or rely heavily on someone's work I cite it and academics can look up all the references if they like and find the sources.

Please do not assume that because I make broad claims and then only cite an earlier summary of my own, that I originated all those ideas and claims. I did not. I am bringing all these ideas from many disciplines together so we can get a new picture of humans and what they do, say, and think. I do not want to interrupt the text by hundreds of references, but please do not get the idea that I believe that I originated everything here.

In fact, the entire theme of this and the other books in the series is that everything we do, say, or think originates in our worlds—our social, societal, cultural, discursive, economic, colonized, patriarchal, and stratified worlds. And that includes my writing these books!

1 Where psychology went wrong 60 years ago

An erroneous turn at the fork in the Gestalt road

For a long time now, psychology has had some unchallenged but wrong assumptions. From all the pre-psychology era and then through the first 100 years of a named 'psychology', the following were assumed to be obviously true by all but a few:

- People function both with a body and also with something else separate and hard to describe—the mind, soul, mentality, consciousness, thoughts, experience.
- The two parts work together in some way but …
- Sometimes the second part has been said to be 'immaterial' and sometimes 'embodied' in some vague way within the body.
- Sensations on our sensory organs are 'taken in' and used to build the mind or 'mental parts', usually said to occur in the brain.
- Thinking is a private process originating deep inside us that no one else can experience.
- We function as individuals in this world.
- What we do originates 'inside us' as choices or decisions, usually taken to mean 'in the brain'.
- Our thinking then determines what we do.

There has also been a hidden history of a few people saying that *all of these assumptions are wrong*.

Turning psychology inside out

In this book I wish to bring together what is wrong with the aforementioned assumptions, and then, more importantly, spend time showing how we can still understand what people do without all that baggage. Doing this changes the whole nature of the 'psychology enterprise' that began in the late 1800s, and will especially change:

- How 'psychology' needs to merge with the other social sciences (V5).
- How we think about and 'treat' the range of 'mental health' issues (V6).

I see the Gestalt theorists, from roughly the 1920s to the 1940s, as pivotal in modern psychology, not so much by what they tried to develop but by the criticisms they raised of the current psychology of that time. Sadly, most of this has been ignored ever since except in a few little pockets of psychology. Other extremely powerful criticisms were also made by others, but were ignored in subsequent discussions of psychology (Bentley, 1935; Guerin, 2016a).

The point will be that the Gestalt theorists posed difficult questions for any 'psychology enterprise', and there were two paths that followed from this 'fork in the road'. I will argue that psychology took the wrong path 60 years ago, based on a mistake to be outlined later in this chapter.

What can we learn from a broken triangle?

As a quick rundown, there were three main characters involved initially in the Gestalt criticisms, Max Wertheimer, Kurt Koffka, and Wolfgang Köhler, from roughly the 1920s to the 1940s. They published articles on some perceptual effects that were immediate and real, as opposed to the sensory experiments that had been taking place in psychology labs all around the world following from Wundt, Titchener, and others. Have a look at the sensory experiment shown in Figure 1.1, which is similar to the other Gestalt demonstrations.

What do you see in Figure 1.1? Answer this first!

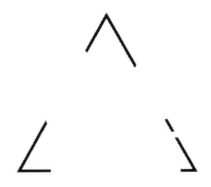

Figure 1.1 The Gestalt triangle sensory experiment

According to the psychology wisdom at that time and also now, light rays make sensations on our retinas of four black lines, some with angles, and our brain *constructs* a triangle from these sensations. But when I ask what you see, however, you see a triangle. A ragged, broken old triangle, but still a triangle. And we see it *immediately*, 100 per cent, without a time lag. We do *not* see four bits of black line and—hey presto!—a few seconds later, we see a constructed triangle.

So, what is the big deal about this? Well, these and other demonstrations like it were all immediate and compelling ("I see a triangle"), with about 100 per cent agreement (unlike the introspective reports of 'sensations'). From this, the Gestaltists argued that *we must see in some bigger organizational units*. What we do as humans is done in terms of bigger units ("I see a triangle"), but we cannot see a triangle just from the immediate sensory-datum of light impinging in the retina. What we 'see' does not appear to be the 'raw' units of elementary sensations. (Caveat: as a very important point that will come up later in this chapter to resolve this puzzle, notice the ambiguity of the word 'see' in this sentence: "We do not see four black lines we see a triangle." Before going on, try to 'draw' what you 'see' above in Figure 1.1. I will come back to this as it shows the mistake that propelled current psychology along the wrong path.)

The work of the Gestaltists started with perceptual phenomena but eventually broadened into the units of everyday social life as well (Kurt Lewin). Koffka (1935) famously used the expression, "The whole is other than the sum of the parts", meaning that adding up all the retinal sensations from the diagram in Figure 1.1, the whole is more—it is a triangle!

Another point from the Gestalt demonstrations was that most work stemming from Wundt and Titchener would have focused on the black lines, aka the black triangle. The white 'background' would not have been thought about. But, the Gestaltists emphasized in their demonstrations that the *background context* was also important in understanding the bigger units being studied (such as triangles). They started talking in terms of 'field' theory, borrowing that word from physics. Answering the question "What do you see?" is not about isolated light waves hitting the retina, but of bigger units *that must also include the field of other events going on at the same time* (I prefer the word 'context' to 'field'). But the problem I will get to next is whether the white background is enough of the context to consider? Are there even more relevant contexts in this simple example? (Spoiler: the social and discursive contexts are actually important also, even in this triangle example.)

None of this meant that physiology was not important. The Gestaltists, like everyone else, made little diagrams of what the brain and neurological circuits might look like in the details of what was available at that time. But for them, there needed to be bigger organizational units *within* the neurological circuitry. And some, like Donald Hebb in 1949, tried to conceptually do something in line with this, with what was known about brain physiology in his slightly later period.

We can also take some of the criticisms further. The Gestaltists emphasized that there was no *passive* reception of sensory input, but that perception was an active and more complex set of events. Later in the chapter we will see James Gibson's (1979) criticism that the majority of perception experiments had the head fixed in place and showed participants static 'stimuli', meaning that real perception was being prevented! This was also true, of course, for Gestalt's own demonstrations, which were two-dimensional, had plain backgrounds with no texture, and were fixed.

The Gestalt criticisms can also be taken even further in a way that will become important later in this book. They argued that the approach used by Wundt was flawed because the method he used of having participants 'introspect' on basic 'elements' of the senses and report their 'experience', was not how real perception works (like our triangle), and the 'units' Wundt and Titchener found were therefore flawed and not real units. Taking this further, the introspection of sensations and reporting on sensory experience, therefore, somehow artificially *created* the 'elements' that were reported. That is, Wundt's participants had been shaped by the experimenters (they were often colleagues and students who were 'trained' to do this 'properly') and any *reporting* on basic sensations was artificial and any 'elements' or 'patterns' found were due to language shaping rather than seeing.

What did the Gestaltists do with this?

Despite the good criticisms and a shake-up for psychology, which I will argue later in the chapter put psychology at an important but mistaken fork in the road, the Gestaltists never galvanized a solid core of theory or methods that lasted. But beyond a few small groups (ecological psychology, field psychology), this never took off in the mainstream. Most psychologists referred to Gestalt theory when making criticisms of what was being done, but without showing how to go forward until the late 1950s and 1960s.

I think a problem was that they never found a way to pursue their own criticisms. They continued to carry out more traditional 'experiments' and not just demonstrations, and there were a lot of *conceptual* attempts to move psychology into a new set of practices. But having stated loudly that the field or context is important, they never went beyond a perceptual field to say what these might look like (except occasionally Kurt Lewin). What was needed was some form of analysis of the actual contexts for human behaviours.

The main conceptual attempt at moving forward made by Gestaltists was to get away from the idea of behaviour as being determined by objects, units, things, and 'stimuli', and arguing that *the whole field or context needs to be taken into account.* This was sometimes called a 'molar' view (e.g. Brunswik, 1950), as opposed to Descartes's push to build from the molecular upwards. This was reflected by Gestaltists in phrases such as: psychology is "the study of behavior in its causal connections with the psychophysical fields" and "behavior in its psychophysical field". Humans do not act and behave in a geographical or microphysics field, but in a "behavioral field".

Of course, this does not help us much unless more is known about *what these fields are and how to track them* (what are the contexts for behaviour?). But it is reflected in the triangle in Figure 1.1—that we do not see precisely defined black bits of a certain physical wavelength of light and a measured shape, but instead we immediately report 'seeing' a triangle, and the white background is part of that happening.

Despite this, I believe that the impact of Gestalt ideas was crucial, and that the elements Gestalt wanted appeared later in different ways, just not in the form in which the Gestaltists of 1920–1940 envisaged. These new additions were never labelled as Gestalt, but they could not have come about without the Gestaltists.

Psychology at a fork in the road: where to from here?

The question from here is about these larger, more complex organized units within which our lives are run: *where does this organization of our life units take place? Inside or outside?*

At this point, and then over the next few decades, there were two broad responses to this question, and these were crucial for how psychology developed next. There was a fork in the road and almost all of psychology went in one direction, which I will call *Pathway 1*. This book is now going back 60 years and taking the other direction of *Pathway 2*, to fulfil the Gestaltist's vision.

Pathway 1

> The complexities of our larger organizational units for living are too complex to come from, or arise out of, the world or environment, and so they must be *constructed or developed inside the organism* using whatever meagre 'input', 'sensory data', or 'information' we can get from the world. We 'fill in' the missing bits of the triangle inside of us in some form or another.

Pathway 2

The complexities or organization of our worlds or environments are *already out there in our environments so we can deal, engage, or interface directly with our complex worlds* and adapt. We do not need to construct anything inside us! We 'fill in' the missing black lines into a bigger unit (a 'triangle') from *what is in our world already*, but not in a way ever imagined by the Gestaltists (I will explain how this is done shortly).

I will briefly outline these two pathways, and then come back to the mistake made by those who followed Pathway 1.

Pathway 1

There are many informal observations, experiences, and gut feelings that lead people to take the first of these pathways at the crossroad. If you believe that all we know comes from the light hitting our two-dimensional retina then it really is a puzzle as to how we report 'seeing' a triangle when it is broken. Even more so, how do we see the world as three-dimensional when what hits our eyes is two-dimensional? Cognitive psychologists later talked about the paucity of 'information' (a subtle word that has a long history and does strategic things to our thinking, see V5.1) that lands on our retina, and in the famous phrase of Jerome Bruner, it *must* be that humans "*go beyond the information given*" (i.e. construct inside them) to represent the complex and larger organizing units of our lives (Bruner, 1973).

This Pathway 1 started early with the Gestaltists themselves (I will gradually show you how you I disagree with all that is said here and give alterative scenarios):

Köhler points out that there is *no direct transmission*, to the perceiver, of physical Gestalt properties present in fellow-organisms or other objects. *All unity* must be *newly constructed in the responder* in accordance with his *intrinsic, "authchthonous" brain dynamics*. The subject is thus seen as basically *out of contact with the dynamics of the environment*.

(Brunswik, 1950, p. 63, my italics)

Examples like the triangle in Figure 1.1 were later used to justify cognitive psychology and other 'inside' approaches. If we say that we see a triangle then where does this come from? The sensory environment does not shape a triangle in perception because the missing lines need to be filled in. So, it was therefore argued that we *must* add or originate the missing environmental information inside the person, probably in the brain somewhere. The environment alone cannot explain calling the image in Figure 1.1 a triangle, the argument went (remember that I will argue the opposite in what follows, however).

(Caveat: notice the word 'must' in the previous Brunswik quote. This is social persuasion not logic, like "It behoves us to ..." But it really means, "I cannot see how this could be otherwise". Those taking Pathway 2 need to show that there is another way to 'see' things, and that Pathway 1 psychologies have just not looked hard enough.)

Those going down Pathway 1, therefore, in almost all cases used their gut feeling to propose that we *must* have 'representations' of our worlds—like a map—before we can do anything. This trail of thinking, which arises only if you believe the organization must be done inside us, therefore requires memory of the world stored inside our heads in some way to build the organizational units like a triangle, and ways of acting to the organized units our brains have computed to do things in our worlds. We *must* have a 'schema' or 'prototype' of a 'triangle' stored inside us to 'see' a whole triangle when it is broken. But all these facets arise from this way of thinking, not from actual observations.

I will discuss later in more detail where Pathway 1 led psychology and how we can correct this (see Chapter 8), but there were three main ways in which those driving along the Pathway 1 fork in the road proceeded, up to the current time. If the complex organizational units *must* be built inside the person (we get the 'triangle' unit from the sensory data being 'processed' internally), then three types of psychology can result from this line of thinking:

1. Go back again to *studying what the brain does* since the brain must be where these more complex organizational units are stored and constructed and so the answers will lie in the brain.
2. Since we cannot see what is going on in the brain, however, then do what the computer people were doing at that time, and *build simulations, models, and theories of what might be going on internally* and try and test these with whatever observable responses can be measured.
3. Just *use the everyday or common language of the bigger units* even if we do not know anything about their reality. Talk using the same words as ordinary people do and do not bother to analyse further. Understand what people do just in terms of how they talk about it: "I see a triangle", "I was feeling angry so I threw a book at him", "His marriage was frustrating his ego since he could not fulfil his boyhood fantasies", "I can remember what my mother's face looks like when I close my eyes". *Treat these as descriptions and explanations rather than analyse them discursively as language use in context.*

I will refer back frequently to these three forms of modern psychology, especially when dealing with 'mental health' (V6.2). But to summarize: if you follow Pathway 1, that our bigger units of behaviour and experience must be constructed inside us because the environmental stimuli do not contain enough to explain, then there are three main ways to do such psychologies:

- The units must originate in the brain and so the answers will lie there if we study it hard enough.
- We must build abstract models and simulations of what *might* be going on in the brain (to get a 'triangle' out of bits of black lines) and try and check these through indirect observations.
- Just use everyday explanations about why humans do what they do, and treat these as if they are accurate descriptions of what we need to study (cf. Graumann & Gergen, 1996).

If you go carefully through any modern psychology textbook you will find that all the explanations contained therein will consist of one or more of these. It is now common to mix these as metaphors, as well as treating just one alone. For example, the following are common:

- This part of the brain is probably where the processes of my cognitive model are taking place.
- This part of the brain is probably where [everyday word of what humans do] takes place, e.g. "This part of the brain is probably where *jealousy* takes place".

Pathway 2

Almost all psychologists took Pathway 1, and this is still the dominant approach across almost all forms of psychology, however different they might look. Most current textbook accounts of psychology are a mixture of neurophysiology, cognitive models of what *might* be going on inside the head to organize the bigger units of human action, and the curious case of using everyday terms and words to 'explain' human behaviours. Freud, for instance, explained with a mix of abstract models (the id, ego, and superego), the use of common everyday words and explanations ("the client was frustrated by ..."), and his own dabbling in possible brain mechanisms (a late 1800s version) for all the models of the unconscious (Freud, 1895/1950).

But there have always been a few who took Pathway 2 and argued that although the brain is important it does not *originate* human behaviour and is not agentive—it is important but just an *interface* for the organism to interact directly with its environments. The key argument was that there is plenty of organization and complexity already out there in the environment or lived world that can control even our most complex and fine-tuned behavioural adaptations (even triangles we will see), but *psychologists have just not looked hard enough for the environmental controls over our actions, talking, and thinking.*

Part of the problem is that we do not 'know' all the environmental features that determine our behaviour, in the sense that we cannot name them all or identify them. A second problem is that it is *easier* to pretend that some agentive event happens inside of us so we only have to model or simulate what *might* be going on; it is much more difficult to research and observe the 'agentive nature' of our complex worlds and this requires different research methodologies. A third problem is that most of those travelling along the dirt track of Pathway 2 believe that it is by actively engaging with our environments that we learn our complex worlds, so experimenting with a constrained organism in context-deprived environments ruins any chance of finding the controlling environments. On the other hand, those taking Pathway 2 must account for the uncanny gut experience that all this stuff takes place inside of us (I will cover this later).

In the next chapter I will discuss in more detail where Pathway 2 led those who went against the mainstream psychologies (Pathway 1). There are five main approaches, but the first is as yet unfulfilled:

- Go back again to *studying what the brain does* but treat the brain as an interface that is not agentive, rather than as a place where all of what we do originates. The structuring of our actions, talking, and thinking are already in the world and we are engaging with that rather than constructing a new version; unfortunately, this is mostly unfulfilled as yet.
- Gibson took this approach just with the study of perception, arguing that there were plenty of ways we could act and react to the environment that could lead to very complex responding, and without needing to build an internal model or representation of the world. He called this *direct perception*, but it requires a lot of collateral changes to the fundamentals of mainstream psychology, so it never became popular (see Chapter 5).
- There were a variety of approaches loosely called 'behaviourism', which in different ways claimed that the environment was agentive in human actions; but only one got close to really studying or describing the complete set of complex human environments; this was the *behaviour analysis* started by Skinner (1938). As I will go through in what

follows, most of the other psychologies called 'behaviourism' were really using Pathway 1, and building abstract models of what takes place inside the organism between simple 'stimuli' and responses.

- More recently a social contextual analysis has built on Gibson's work and the most advanced form of behaviourism, but also included all of the *contextual social sciences*, to try and include how all human complex environments or contexts are agentive of our actions (Guerin, 2016b). We need to go beyond the Gestaltists, and our 'fields' must include social, political, discursive, patriarchal, economic, cultural, and opportunity contexts or environments, not simple 'stimuli' devoid of context.

- Some discourse analyses work along similar lines with just the use of language; language must be studied as a behaviour in context and what we say depends upon our social and discursive communities as contexts, not on the way our brain works. Other discourse analyses, however, are very much Pathway 1 and even have associated cognitive models and the use of everyday terms as explanations (I have yet to see a form of discourse analysis with an associated brain model, but I am waiting).

So, in the story I am putting forward that follows from the criticisms of psychology by Gestalt psychologists, there is a major division based around the following:

- Whether there is not enough in our environments to control our finely tuned and complex actions and so somewhere inside of us (usually the brain) we must originate representations or models of the world in order to behave.

- Or whether the determiners of human action, talk, and thinking can arise from the complex lifeworlds in which we are embedded, especially if we include social, societal, and other contexts.

On both sides there are what I have been referring to as 'gut experiences' that their pathway is correct, so attempts by the other pathway must be able to also account for these. For example, we all have gut feelings or gut experiences that our 'thoughts' are not controlled by the immediate environments around us, and that our thoughts *must* be inside of us (that is, we cannot imagine otherwise). This does not mean Pathway 1 is correct, just that these sorts of experience make it more plausible. Which means that anyone arguing for Pathway 2 must be able to show how these gut feelings can arise in other ways (see Chapters 2 and 4).

Where current psychology went wrong: back to the triangle, but from the outside

So how can the 'outside' approaches taking Pathway 2 account for the triangle demonstration and what is found? How can saying "I see a triangle" possibly be shaped by things external to us? It turns out after 60–70 years to be quite simple once you broaden the idea of fields or contexts!

A Gestalt or contextual approach should look for what is actually being done here in *all contexts* (or fields), and this is where the mistake was made. There are, in fact, *two behaviours from two different contexts* in response to the question, "What do you see?":

1. Imagine I had shown you the broken triangle and had first asked you, "Draw this for me". The main field or context for responding to this particular (but still social) question is the original drawing itself of the broken triangle, and we can copy and draw that quite easily and *no one adds the missing bits of the triangle*. I have tried this with classes, and everyone draws the four lines and not a completed triangle. The drawing you make is shaped or contextualized by social instructions and the original 'triangle' picture itself with all its flaws. *All external.*

2. The second context and response to "What do you see?" is *a social request for a verbal response*. The actual external context, field, or environment for this response is *not* the picture and the four bits of black lines but the social relationship you have with the person who is asking. Answering this social question in our normal contexts is *not* about giving an accurate description of what is in front of you, unless your social context had been your art professor and you knew they were trying to trick you to get you to draw accurately.

   This is a bit like when we ask people "Hi! How are you?" and we are not really requesting a detailed description of how they actually are, we are just making social conversation. You would normally answer with a quick standard answer ("I'm fine, thanks"), or perhaps add a little bit of a story if, and only if, it was entertaining: "I'm fine, thanks for asking. Although I did have a problem this morning when a truck ran over my car!" This question is more like a conversation starter and the context is about maintaining your social relationship, not giving your actual health status (called 'phatic communication' in the social sciences).

   So the social contexts are very important in the Gestalt demonstrations, because you respond differently with different social or societal contexts:

an art professor, a friend, or an experimenter. This is no different than giving a different answer to "How are you?" if your *doctor* had asked you this question (of course, you still might not tell the truth!). Or, if you wanted to *test* a social relationship with a friend, you might give a 15-minute monologue about your health.

So, when the Gestaltists asked "What do you see?" the context or environment for answering was a casual social context, and "I see a triangle" was *a perfectly acceptable social reply* but not an accurate description. We are *shaped by our social worlds* to do this all the time. In asking "What do you see?" we have been thoroughly shaped by our (external!) social contexts to give answers like "I saw a dog", even though we hardly saw most of the dog, we could not see the dog's legs at all (we were above the dog), and we could not even tell you details about the dog 'we saw'.

The above provides an 'outside' version (Pathway 2) of why we 'say' we saw a triangle. If the context or field is not social in this way, we can easily 'draw' what is in front of us quite accurately. We do not need to construct any internal representations of triangles to do either of these behaviours, it is all happening *externally* as a casual social–verbal interaction or as a request to draw four black lines in front of us. Change the black lines into a broken circle and we draw differently; have an art professor ask what you see, and you will describe four little black lines, not a 'triangle', so you do not get in trouble. The social contexts should not be excluded from this demonstration, and that was the mistake made.

The above also highlights how the common use of everyday words in psychology to explain human behaviour can be very misleading. There are ambiguities in the word 'see' in the original triangle demonstrations that are missed but that lead us to imagine that we need to construct a triangle inside of us to do the behaviour of saying "I see a triangle":

- We do not 'see a black triangle' in any perceptual sense, since we can easily draw the broken triangle accurately in a perceptual sense when the context is there.
- We can socially name "I saw a triangle" if the context is just a casual social interaction for which the four black lines are not important (in fact, you can be a 'smart-arse' if you answer "four black lines" to the question when it is a casual social interaction).

Both these can be accounted for by *shaping from the external world*, one from the black lines and one from our normal social context of answering simple questions. There never was any need for Pathway 1.

A bit more about Pathway 1: neuropsychology, cognitive psychologies, and the many psychologies based on everyday terms

We have seen that there were three main responses to the Gestalt criticisms, each of which kept the idea that everything that makes us do what we do happens inside us. Two of the three had been there all along in both psychology and in the general public, but the cognitive approach was new and quickly took over psychology with the rise of computer simulations:

1. Study neurophysiology more intensively as the main focus.
2. Make models, theories, and simulations of what is going on inside the head, which narrowed down to cognitive psychology.
3. Use the everyday language of internal causes to 'do' psychology.

Pretty much everything that has happened in the last 75 years of mainstream psychology (textbooks) has come from these three responses (Brunswik, 1950, is an early attempt to integrate and 'unify' these approaches even prior to cognitive psychology, while not changing the main assumptions). Most academics focused on the first two, while the therapists, counsellors, and 'soft' academics (humanists, etc.) focused on the third.

My real point is that *no one was able to think in a different way*. This was not a matter of following good data but of being unable to reconceptualize these three approaches. The data collected in support of the cognitive theories was extremely general and indirect, made up of averages, single observations of loose measurements, and was able to be interpreted in many other ways if the thinking to do so had been there. I am optimistic that the brain observations we already have can be rethought in terms of just an interface that also uses the head and body, rather than as creators of anything.

This is also the problem for you, the reader! The alternatives I am going to present later go against your very own common ways of talking about, and 'explaining', why people do what they do. Most of our daily talk and the media (as well as psychology) places everything agentive in the head as the 'explanation'. And I am hoping to show you better ways to think about your life paths and why you do what you do by getting a better idea of your nuanced external contexts.

The rise and rise of neuropsychology

The main change in neuropsychology has been the huge developments in understanding the brain since the early days of Wundt, Titchener, and the all learning theorists, who knew little back then. So much has been discovered that is of real importance, and yet conceptual errors have crept in because of the assumptions of Pathway 1:

- First, each new discovery of neuropsychology (which are real) has been extrapolated along the way to explain far more than it is able.
- Second, the trend has been to see each new development as showing how the brain *originates* what people do. This is achieved (wrongly) by thinking of sensory input, and treating this sensory input as something that goes 'inside' the organism for the brain to do its stuff on, and *originate* as an *agent* what the organism then does based on this.
- We need to treat the magic of the brain as an interface for acting and adapting to the world, and this means putting *the world* forward as the key originator and agent of what we do. As we will see and as pointed out by Gibson (1979), it is responding to changes on the retina that is important, not the 'sensations'.

The real problem here is not the neuropsychologists, on the whole, but the popular writers and lay public who now use brain discourses to supposedly 'explain' everything. Try going into your local bookshop and look in the psychology section. There are books about your 'athletic brain' and how it can improve your sporting abilities, about how when you meditate it changes your brain, how you can eat chocolate and the changes in your behaviour are because of your brain. The brain is fast becoming the only agent a person needs anymore. Apparently, everything starts in the brain!

Early (and later) cognitivisms

What we now call the approach of cognitive psychology had two major starting points at different times (more in Chapter 8). The first came from the frustrations of some early academics working with stimulus–response behaviourisms, and the second from advances in computing and especially computer simulations of human behaviour. As new developments were made in computing science, these were sequentially adapted into cognitive psychology to try and explain why people do what they do, but as models.

My account here differs (once again) from the typical psychology textbooks. In the latter, all forms of 'behaviourism' are lumped together even though they differ markedly. I will be making the division along the lines of the Gestaltists' fork in the road, and whether what were labelled as 'behaviourisms' promoted that what humans do *originates* inside the organism or in the environment.

All behaviourisms are given that title because they study *what an organism does that we can see.* Some did this, however, because even though they believed that what we do originates inside of us, they knew that we cannot see what is going on inside of us so, *necessarily*, we have to just look at what an organism can be seen to be doing. These groups are early versions of cognitivism and follow Pathway 1. They observe overt behaviours because we cannot see inside people where it supposedly all originates. The other group of 'behaviourists' look at what can be observed of both the organism and the environment/context/field within which it is embedded, and these follow Pathway 2 (they will be discussed in the next chapter) (see Table 1.1).

Table 1.1 Types of behaviourism

Type of 'behaviourism'	Main reason for being behavioural	What this led to later

S–R behaviourisms
Behavioural learning
  theories
Purposive behaviourism
  (Tolman)
Hull–Spence
  behaviourism
	The origin, determining nature, or agentive nature of what organisms do primarily occurs *inside* the organism
	But we cannot see this happening so instead we can only observe what the organism does in certain (stimulus) conditions and either guess (in everyday language) or theoretically model what is going on inside
		Cognitive psychology
		Animal cognition
		Some behaviour modification

Radical
  behaviourism ideas
Operant behaviourism
Parts of Watsonian
  behaviourism
Arthur F. Bentley
	The origin, determining nature, or agentive nature of what organisms do, primarily occurs *outside* the organism
	We observe *both* what the organism does in different environmental conditions *and what the environment does when the organism acts*
		Behaviour analysis
		Social contextual analysis
		Discourse analysis (some)

Stimulus–response behaviourisms

The stimulus–response behaviourisms (S–R) developed out of the reflex arc idea and the many different versions of learning theories that came from Thorndike. The idea was that 'connections' or 'networks' were formed *inside* the organism between stimuli and responses, and that this is where responses *originated*. Learning was just about building up lots of connections inside the organism.

Such positions became called 'behaviourism' because, exactly like cognitive psychology later, they realized that they could only look at or observe what the organism did, not what it was deciding, or perceiving, or thinking. Those events could not be seen even though they were the main determining agents in what happened next according to these views. Thorndike's laws of behaviour, for example, occurred inside the organism and could not be directly observed, and only the *outward manifestations* of an *inside process* could be observed.

To highlight the later contrast to Gibson, notice that from Wundt onwards and including all the S–R behaviourists it had always been assumed that for organisms to function they must *take something in* through the senses (sensory data, later 'information'). But once something is taken in, then obviously the main action or agency will occur on the inside. However, Gibson's model of perception and sensation, as we will see in Chapter 5, allowed that organisms could perceive and see *without having to take anything inside at all*. So all these problems then disappear, puff!

There appeared, therefore, a whole hodgepodge of S–R theories in the next few decades after Gestalt, which worked with this logic and thinking. Details differed, but the main gist followed what is written above. Not read by most psychologists, Arthur F. Bentley made an impressive 'deconstruction' of the 1930 and 1935 theories and showed how these, and other, errors were part of all these theories (Bentley, 1935; Guerin, 2016a).

Tolman's (1932) work was a strong bridge to cognitive psychology. He worked with rats and on how they learned to run in mazes. Like Thorndike, he found that they did not learn suddenly through insight but became faster over time. However, he also got frustrated because, like the Gestaltists, he could see larger patterns occurring and having to explain all this in precise and immediately present 'stimulus conditions' did not seem a good way forward. So, he moved (as per earlier in this chapter, discursive strategy 3, see p. 13) to use common, everyday terms for 'explaining' what the rats were doing 'inside' their brains. It became known as 'purposive behaviourism' because it seemed that rats developed 'higher units' or 'plans' inside them as they learned. 'Purpose' was the everyday term he took to be transparent, while "plan' was used later, as we will see.

Tolman's position was put most simply and directly in the following:

> [*The brain*] is far more like a map control room than it is like an old-fashioned telephone exchange. The *stimuli*, which are *allowed in*, are not *connected* by just simple one-to-one switches to the *outgoing* responses. Rather, the *incoming impulses* are usually *worked over* and *elaborated* in the central control room into a tentative, *cognitive-like map of the environment*. And it is this tentative map, indicating routes and paths and environmental relationships, which finally *determines what responses*, if any, the animal will finally *release*.
>
> (Tolman, 1948, p. 192, my italics)

This quote shows the combination of Gestalt bigger units, everyday, and very abstract talk about internal thinking, and how internal cognitions lead to the (agentive) responses that are 'released' (a curious but interesting word to use). If you read this as a discursive analysis it is extremely revealing. Note the words I have put in italics. Pathway 2 says that all those words are mistaken!

The beginnings of cognitive psychology

By the 1960s, the seeds of cognitive psychology were in place. There was dissatisfaction that S–R behaviourisms were not getting a grip on big units of human behaviour, the development of computers and simulation of human behaviours by computers was rapidly advancing, and the meticulous false precision (pretending to be science by having fancy equations for rat maze behaviour) from some of the S–R behaviourisms (Hull, 1943) was getting tiresome to many.

What happened next was not a breakthrough in evidence or data. It was *professional acquiescence* to several ideas that allowed for Pathway 1 and the three subsequent discourses to seem real (brain, abstract models, and the use of everyday language explanations). What I mean is that nothing new was 'found out', but academic psychologists started going along with, allowing, or acquiescing to, abstract modelling of what might be going on 'inside' humans, and the use of everyday terms to explain human behaviour (and even rat behaviour!). Here are the main ideas everyone went along with:

- For bigger human units of behaviour we are not going to quickly get the neurophysiological evidence so instead we should use another real 'scientific' method of working, i.e. *build models* of what might be going on inside people, when we cannot observe directly (as was assumed wrongly).

- The control of behaviour could not possibly come from just the environment alone, and in Bruner's (1973) words, humans therefore "need to go beyond the information given".
- The 'stimuli' talked about in S–R behaviourisms were too simple for real life, but the response to this was *not* to study our real worlds closer and contextually, but to get more complicated models.
- Everything comes from a two-dimensional image on the retina so, in order to go beyond the information given, somewhere in the brain we must *construct* that third dimension and build a new representation of the world.
- Our engagement with the world therefore becomes *ipso facto* our engagement with our internal representations of the world.
- For the computer simulations, there was an extra assumption that if a simulation output matched some observed human behaviour then that simulation must be something like what is going on inside humans (not logically correct, however).

As we will see in the next chapter, all of these assumptions have been disputed but they were taken for granted in that era (*professional acquiescence*). On a more practical level, from the messy research with trying to make precise 'scientific' measurements of rat behaviour, drive states, and stimuli, researchers were given permission (*professional acquiescence*) to wax lyrical about *possible* models and theories of what *might* be going on in the head (using 'modal hedges' in discourse analysis terms). Data was typically collected as single-point measurements abstracted from the real substance, and this was justified by another assumption (going back to Descartes!) that this was necessary and we will be progressing towards building up the bigger units from the smaller foundational cognitive units.

Miller, Galanter, and Pribram (1960)

One of the first attempts to move on from all this was the publication of Miller et al.'s (1960) *Plans and the Structure of Behavior*. These authors were certainly envisaging the bigger units of human behaviour à la Gestalt and talked about these as 'plans' that we 'have' and that we follow. This clearly brings in the computer analogy: "The notion of a Plan that guides behavior is, again not entirely accidentally, quite similar to the notion of a program that guides an electronic computer" (Miller et al., 1960, p. 2). They also expressed the problem and frustration of S–R behaviourisms not being able to deal with bigger human units of behaviour:

To psychologists who like alternatives to nickel-in-the-slot, stimulus-response conceptions of man ... (It is so reasonable to insert between the stimulus and the response a little wisdom. And there is no particular need to apologize for putting it there, because it was already there before psychology arrived.)

(Miller et al., 1960, p. 2)

Instead of mathematical equations trying to predict the maze behaviour of a rat, they wanted more like this:

Consider how an ordinary day is put together. You awaken, and as you lie in bed, or perhaps as you move slowly about in a protective shell of morning habits, you think about what the day will be like—it will be hot, it will be cold; there is too much to do, there is nothing to fill the time; you promised to see him, she may be there again today. If you are compulsive, you may worry about fitting it all in, you may make a list of all the things you have to do. Or you may launch yourself into the day with no clear notion of what you are going to do or how long it will take. But, whether it is crowded or empty, novel or routine, uniform or varied, your day has a structure of its own—it fits into the texture of your life. And as you think what your day will hold, you construct a plan to meet it. What you expect to happen foreshadows what you expect to do.

(Miller et al., 1960, p. 5)

This clearly mixes Pathway 1 discourses 2 and 3 (see pp. 13), although the authors bring in the brain (discourse 1, see p. 13) later in their book. They mostly mix simple abstract modelling (their test–operate–test–exit (TOTE) unit) with the use of everyday words (*habits, think, promised, compulsive, worry, launch, construct, expect*).

They also had the strong assumption that if you can model actions for a computer then that must be what humans do:

A plan is, for an organism, essentially the same as a program for a computer, especially if the program has the sort of hierarchical character described above. Newell, Shaw, and Simon have explicitly and systematically used the hierarchical structure of lists in their development of "information-processing languages" that are used to program high-speed digital computers to simulate human thought processes. Their success in this direction—which the present authors find most impressive and encouraging—argues strongly for the hypothesis that a hierarchical structure is the basic form of organization in human problem-solving.

(Miller et al., 1960, p. 16)

Apart from the logical errors in this, some years later computing brought in parallel processing models and other innovations that eschewed their less-flexible 'hierarchical structures'. Cognitive psychology followed suit. All were equally fictitious models of what might be going on in a human if the brain actually did control behaviour.

Finally, they saw that this led to having internal representations and went along with it because they believed the environment was insufficient to control the details and complexity of human behaviour: "A human being—and probably other animals as well—builds up an internal representation, a model of the universe, a schema, a simulacrum, a cognitive map" (Miller et al., 1960, p. 7). Again, this is persuasion and acquiescence rather than observations, and is plausible due to a limited idea of 'stimulus' inherited, ironically, from the S–R behaviourists. We saw earlier how the Gestalt triangle example could be explained by the external uses of language, and 'cognition' mostly turns out to be language use, in fact (see Chapters 4 and 8).

For example, they use an example of the sentence, "They are flying planes". Their point was that while the sequence of phonemes (the 'stimulus') was unchanged, the two possible analyses "(They) (are flying) (planes)" and "(They) (are) (flying planes)" are very different. But notice that this is a very simplistic notion of stimulus or environment and they had forgotten the Gestalt idea of *field*. The two 'analyses' have very different contexts in their history but what is presented here *is* ambiguous. We would respond in everyday life based on a lot more context that has been removed. Indeed, different languages rely more or less on context beyond the words or symbols themselves (such as Mandarin).

The problem here is the same as Gibson (1979) later pointed out for the use of perceptual illusions in psychology: they all consisted of ambiguous drawings (a vase or two faces) but this does not mean that our response must be constructed in the brain. The real world has features (invariants, context) that tell us to respond either as a vase or as two faces, without any internal constructions, but the illusion demonstration has removed all context, so this is ambiguous and context deprived. It is like being trained with your friends to tell one version of a story and another version to your parents, and then having friends and parents come together and ask you to tell the story! *The confusion and ambiguity is already there in the external environment*. This is equivalent to what "They are flying planes" has done—removed all context, shown that what people 'say' is confused, and conclude that therefore it must be constructed in the head. Not so. If we add context, there are no issues.

Later cognitive models

The later cognitive models took a slightly different approach and emphasized the whole processing of 'sensory data' that is 'taken inside'. This was very

stimulus → receptor → afferent nerve → connective fibres → efferent nerve → effector response

Figure 1.2 Early reflex arc idea

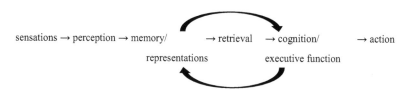

sensations → perception → memory/   → retrieval   → cognition/   → action
representations   executive function

Figure 1.3 Pattern of cognitive models

much in the tradition of Wundt and Titchener but with more precision (albeit theoretical and abstract modelling). It was also very much like the early reflex arc ideas but made a bit more modern. Figure 1.2 shows the early reflex arc idea.

Figure 1.3 shows the broad pattern of cognitive models.

Both Figures 1.2 and 1.3 incorporate the same major assumptions of 'internal' models of human behaviour, and most of the assumptions given right at the start of this chapter. Something is taken 'in' through the senses, which might be nerve impulses or 'information'. This is processed in a cognitive centre or brain process, and representations of the 'outside world' made and then stored. Future processing will include the retrieval and use of these representations *in order to* make responses. The real difference is that for the cognitive model there are more details (albeit all theoretical and modelled) given of the 'connective fibres'. The memory is the same associative or neural networks. Our life then consists of *engaging with these representations* rather than directly with the world.

What we need to question here are things like: how much of this was simply word changes (jargon, models)? What happened to the environment and its analysis in all this? Did everyone stop observing the actual environments? What happened to responding or actions? Could you really test these proposed 'units' of models? What exactly is the material and social status of 'information'? Is anything really 'taken in' by the system? For example, if, as Gibson (1979) claimed (see Chapter 5), there is nothing actually 'taken in' through the senses in order to see, then the whole processing model is mistaken. Or if there is enough in the environment to see without needing to go 'beyond the information given', then the whole processing model falls over. But it was only ever made out of abstract promises.

Psychologies of everyday terms

Apart from the attempts to sound scientific, almost all the psychologies have used our everyday talking and explanations for human behaviour as their basic discourse (like the uses of 'purpose' and 'plan' discussed earlier). How we humans use language will play a major part in this book, and language has also been very misrepresented in the past. We have seen its double role in the 'triangle' example (see Figure 1.1); so much of what current psychology treats as its 'observations' is really talking, which really needs to be analysed as social discourse instead. There are several reasons for its importance, which can be summarized now so you can start thinking this through:

- How we use language is what really makes us different from other animals.
- How we use language is what makes 'the body' seem different to something else in human life—the mind, soul, mentality, consciousness, thoughts, experience—but each of these are the body using language rather than something non-material.
- What is labelled 'cognition' is really about language use with its special properties.
- How we use language allows us new 'virtual' environments and this can shape behaviours not seen in other animals (but we will see later how these 'virtual' environments of language use are really based in material reality, see Chapter 3).
- How we use language is also what can really mess our lives up and is a large part of our conflicts and 'mental health' issues.

So, the role of language in our lives will begin early in the book and continue throughout. I will show how language actually originates externally in our *social* environments as Pathway 2 (and is both external and material) and not *inside* us, and that this is what allows all the weird, wonderful, and virtual properties that both help and hinder us. For example, a sizeable proportion of 'mental health' symptoms are about talking and thinking, which are both products of language use.

What I will also show is that most of the human actions for which we (and psychologists like Jerome Bruner) simply *cannot see* a 'cause' in the outside world (and so they *must* invent metaphors of the 'inside'), are really phenomena of language. *'Cognitive' phenomena are language phenomena and are external, to be found along the other fork in Pathway 2.*

Our everyday words are dangerous for understanding what we do

What I want to emphasise about language here in Chapter 1 is that we need to be very careful about the everyday words we use when *explaining* human actions, talking, and thinking. These words have developed out of everyday language practices and hinder us from thinking about things differently (like "I see a triangle"). What I have done in this chapter, in fact, is a partial discourse analysis of the discourses of psychology and how they have developed along with the discursive strategies that have been used to argue for Pathway 1 psychologies.

Everyday ways of talking and explaining are (socially) useful short cuts for when we do not know what is really going on or we are having informal casual social interactions. The discursive goal is to keep the social relationship going rather than to be accurate (like our triangle). So rather than nothing, we can talk about 'deciding' to wear our blue coat, or not treading on the cat because we saw it and made sure we avoided it. These are fine for everyday life.

And I do not want you to change these everyday words in your everyday life and conversation—that would just sound pretentious. If the day were to come in the future when everyone agreed that we must refer to our environments or lifeworlds instead of our 'inner' selves when explaining human behaviour, then we might be able to change these in everyday use as well. But if you do so now you will lose your friends. No one will have any idea what you are talking about.

What I am saying here is that we learn all our words and the ways we talk in order to build common shorthand usages, and these *very frequently use 'inside' words to make things easier for social conversation* (we do not have to explain very much that way). Other groups get a little closer by explaining not as things happening inside us, but as external 'spirits' or other entities. Our easy explanations by using events 'inside us' are *the equivalent* in fact of using 'external' non-material entities to explain things when we do not know what is really happening.

The real problem to mention here, however, is that once we accept common-sense or everyday ways of talking, we then come to assume that *they are what needs explaining* in psychology. And this is usually wrong! For example, if we assume, as most people do, that 'we' originate our thoughts *inside* of us, then clearly this is what psychology must explain under the topic of 'the psychology of thinking'. It might not occur to people that the psychology of thinking might look completely different to how we talk in everyday life (see Chapter 4). Box 1.1 includes some common everyday terms that are fine for everyday life 'explanations', but disastrous if we assume these are true and need explaining by psychology.

The real point is that language use and thinking in our lives is directed at affecting people (see Chapters 3 and 4) and so these ways of talking and thinking are not related to any 'truth' about people and how they work. They are mostly explanations that are 'socially satisfying' rather than true, and they suffice for doing things to your regular everyday social relationships.

Box 1.1   Common everyday terms for everyday life 'explanations'

Thinking	Perceive	See
Behaving	Underlying	Mechanisms
Deciding	Adaptive	Associations
Choosing	Associative networks	Brain causes
Processing	Subjective/objective	Culture
Private	Biological basis	Receptors
Deep	Awareness	Social
Neural networks	Dispositions	Hard-wired
Inner–outer	Internal	Conscious/unconscious
Evolutionary		

But using them to base our whole talking about and explaining human behaviour in psychology is very problematic. We will come back to this problem repeatedly.

References

Bentley, A. F. (1935). *Behavior knowledge fact.* Bloomington, IN: Principia Press.

Bruner, J. (1973). *Beyond the information given: Studies in the psychology of knowing.* New York, NY: W. W. Norton & Company.

Brunswik, E. (1950). *The conceptual framework of psychology.* Chicago, IL: University of Chicago Press.

Freud, S. (1895/1950). Project for a scientific psychology. In J. Strachey (Ed.), *The standard edition of the complete works of Sigmund Freud, volume 1* (pp. 283–343). London: Hogarth Press.

Gibson, J. J. (1979). *An ecological approach to visual perception.* Boston, MA: Houghton Mifflin.

Graumann, C. E., & Gergen, K. J. (Eds.) (1996). *Historical dimensions of psychological discourse.* Cambridge, UK: Cambridge University Press.

Guerin, B. (2016a). Arthur F. Bentley's early writings: His relevance to behavior analysis, contemporary psychology and the social sciences. *Revista Perspectivas em Análise do Comportamento, 7,* 1–35.

Guerin, B. (2016b). *How to rethink human behavior: A practical guide to social contextual analysis.* London: Routledge.

Hebb, D. O. (1949). *The organization of behavior.* New York, NY: Wiley.

Hull, C. L. (1943). *Principles of behavior: An introduction to behavior theory.* New York, NY: Appleton-Century-Crofts.

Koffka, K. (1935). *Principles of Gestalt psychology.* London: Routledge & Kegan Paul.

Miller, G. A., Galanter, E., & Pribram, K. H. (1960). *Plans and the structure of behavior.* New York, NY: Holt, Rinehart & Winston.

Skinner, B. F. (1938). *The behavior of organisms.* New York, NY: Appleton-Century-Crofts.

Tolman, E. C. (1932). *Purposive behavior in animals and men.* New York, NY: Century Co.

Tolman, E. C. (1948). Cognitive maps in rats and men. *Psychological Review, 55,* 189–208.

2 Going back to the 'fork in the road' and starting a fresh contextual approach

While the mainstream psychologies currently stay on the Pathway 1 road of the previous chapter, there have always been a few people, not very popular in the mainstream and very misunderstood, who have pursued Pathway 2. Recall that the idea for Pathway 2 is that the worlds we live in are worlds of plenty of details and complexity and we do not need to construct representations at all, and not 'inside the head', whatever that means. We see, act, talk, and even think *directly* with our environments, even if in very complex ways. And the way we materially engage directly with our (social and discursive) worlds with language use replaces the abstract 'cognitive' models. Pathway 2 stipulates that all we do is entirely possible by interacting and adapting directly with the world. In fact, Gibson (see later in the chapter) called his work *direct perception.* Finally, most of the problems arise because talking about an event is confused with the event itself, like the triangle in Chapter 1.

All of the people and schools of thought in Pathway 2 still believe that the brain is important, but they do not believe that what we do, say, or think *originates* in the brain—the brain is not an agent but more like an *interface.* If something is creative or complex, then that arises from the world itself; it is not created or given complexity inside the brain. Chapter 4 will demonstrate how thinking arises from our external contexts. We saw the example in Chapter 1 of the Gestalt triangle that seemed complex (saying "triangle" when the shape was incomplete, and thereby triggering the cognitive revolution), but I showed that the complexity was in the environment all along. We just needed to look more closely and see that a *social context* was significant as well as the triangle shape.

The other common feature of Pathway 2 positions is that we must also take into account how *our actions, talking, and even thinking affect and change our worlds so that our worlds are constantly changing because of what we do.* So, for Gibson, seeing *is* moving and doing, and these change our world and therefore affect what we will 'see' next. For Skinner, acting on the world produces changes in that world that greatly affect us and our *next* actions. For discourse analysis, what we say in context not only affects people but what they do then affects what we also say and do next.

So, all of our seeing, acting, talking, and thinking directly changes our worlds (even if it is just that we move a little or not say what we could of) and this is vitally important to understanding why we do what we do (and what we do next). Again, Pathway 1 research that studies the 'reactions' to passive stimuli miss all of this because what we do (typically we say something) does not change that world but only the internal stuff.

The onus on Pathway 2, therefore, is to show that there are sufficient variations, nuances, and complexities in the environment/context/field to allow the complexity, nuances, and adaptations of human behaviour, and that our worlds and environments have sufficient complexity and adaptations to change when we do. As we will see, the common problem with both Pathway 1 and Pathway 2 is that neither has properly taken into account the complexities and adaptations to our *social and societal environments*, and how *they* change when we act, talk, or think. This is where the really complex things occur, especially talking and thinking (which are what is now called cognition). But this lack of exploring our environments is exactly what the Pathway 1 approach took as evidence that the environment cannot account for what humans do.

We will now look at the main contextual approaches of Pathway 2, and their limitations from not exploring and observing all of the contexts of our worlds.

Gibson and direct perception

In 1955, James and Eleanor Gibson produced a remarkable paper that got lost through the 'cognitive revolution'. The paper was called "Perceptual Learning: Differentiation or Enrichment?" and while it was simple, it heralded a major shift in thinking that never became well known. James Gibson expanded and explored these ideas throughout his career, but unfortunately, he was either ignored or his ideas were interpreted wrongly in terms of cognitive models.

Gibson argued against a basic assumption that had been unchallenged through all the history of psychology and even before—that "something is taken in by the sensory organs". Once you believe that, then all the complex organizing of the world, and our adaptations to the world, must obviously be done inside the head or the mind.

For Gibson, this assumption was incorrect despite its long history and the way it is also assumed in common-sense talk. He argued instead that we respond differentially to *changes or differences*, we do not respond to

a 'stimulus' or a 'sensation' (cf. Deleuze, 1994). Ignore our human complexity for the moment and think about a plant that moves towards the sun—
a phototrophic plant (but not moving like a triffid). If you change the plant's
position in your room, within a few days the plant has moved its leaves
to face the sun. If we forget for the moment that most of us are a bit more
complex than plants, how can they do this without forming a representation
of the sun? Do they need to 'take in' information and store a representation
of the sun? Do they need to respond to the sun as an object—'the sun'?
Clearly, they do not.

The same thinking, therefore, is what Gibson (and Skinner as it will
turn out) were all about. In their original paper, Gibson and Gibson (1955)
proposed that learning to see happens by finer and finer *differentiations* of
behaviour or doing things, rather than by 'enriching' the 'image' found on
the sensory organs when light or sound falls on them. Can you see that what
they meant by 'enrichment' was precisely what (as we saw in the previous
chapter) Jerome Bruner (1973) later called 'going beyond the information given'? This is the cognitive idea that the environment cannot provide
enough on the retina for complex behaviours to occur, so the brain must
have to *add more* by doing something called 'processing'.

The Gibson's were basically disagreeing with this and were saying (way
back in 1955!) that you have simply not looked hard enough. Mainstream
psychology disagreed with Gibson and Gibson so their idea was sunk
beneath the huge increase in cognitive models and computer simulations
that followed. Occasionally over the intervening years, some tried to make
cognitive models of what Gibson meant but these attempts missed the whole
radical point of what he was trying to say.

Luckily for us, Gibson did not give up when cognitivists missed his point
entirely but kept working on what had to come next—a thorough exploration
of *what differences and effects our environments can provide* to shape our
perceptual behaviours, especially the complex ones—how does our seeing/
moving change our visual environments? We will see in what follows that
this was also what Skinner began, but he was interested in more than just perception, which was Gibson's focus. The *consequential differences* that are
available from interacting with our environments were called *affordances*
by Gibson and *consequences* or *contingencies* by Skinner. Both of them
only managed some of this exploration (they were only human, after all),
and both left out details of all the many fine differences and discriminations
that our social, cultural, economic, and other worlds afford us. That is what
we need to do now.

I will leave the reader to follow up details of Gibson's 'perceptual
systems' and there is more on this in Chapter 5. The aim was to show
that there were enough differences in the world (when we move or act in

some way) to afford what we do with our eyes. For example, if you look at a patterned carpet then the size of the patterns on the carpet get smaller the further away they are from you. Moreover, if you move around, these whole displays change also according to distance. Here, then, are perfect *differences* occurring 'on the retina' that are three-dimensional (over time and movement), and so we can respond differently to near and far by moving rather than by 'inner processing' or enrichment.

Gibson also really looked closely at how *textures* in our environment could shape us to respond differently (to see differentially, that is). If we study moving organisms with moving eye parts that are in a textured or complex environment (not a flat white background), then *three dimensions are available on the retina* to respond with interactively. There was never any need for the brain to *construct* a three-dimensional representation and store it away somewhere. We can respond immediately and directly in three dimensions if we (1) respond as a moving organism, (2) to *changes* on the retina rather than 'images' (3) over time, and in (4) a complex or textured environment.

Gibson also wrote very importantly about the differences in artwork and hallucinations to regular perception (more in Chapter 5). Moving, for example, has less impact with artwork and hallucinations so we respond differently to them than we do to the 'real thing'. And to remember the main point here: *all those complexities to which we can respond differentially with different outcomes or affordances are out there in our environments, they are not constructed or enriched inside our heads!*

You should now be able to piece together Gibson's criticisms of most experimental research in psychology. The 'stimuli' used are devoid of texture or context (even our triangle), they are stripped bare in the name of experimental control so all the myriad changes we normally can respond to are gone, including movement. Without movement, most 'seeing' of three dimensions is gone. Likewise, as mentioned earlier, visual illusions were used as evidence that stimuli needed to be enriched because they are ambiguous when we look at them (a vase or two faces? a rabbit or a white duck?). But without the texture and movement, of course it is ambiguous. But this does not prove that we need cognitive processing to provide more than is in the environment.

Skinner and environmental behaviourisms

We saw in the last chapter that there were many forms of behaviourism. Most arose because people could not see the internal working of the brain that they assumed originated human behaviour, so they had to stick to observing what could be seen on the outside. They were really Pathway 1 theorists, however.

There was one who was different and much more radical, and indeed he called the philosophy of what he was doing exactly that: radical behaviourism. This was B. F. Skinner, who arguably has been the most misrepresented of modern psychologists. Most textbooks and books about the history of psychology just plainly get Skinner wrong! This is similar to what Gibson went through but some of Skinner's conceptual writings got academics more fired up, and one serious attack was very influential in allowing academics to ignore totally what Skinner was proposing (*professional acquiescence* again!). This more vicious attack by Noam Chomsky actually missed the point and he was really attacking the other forms of S–R behaviourism mentioned earlier, which ironically were the very ones that led to cognitive psychology.

I do not have room to give a fair account of Skinner's work here but will highlight a few points, and much is already incorporated into social contextual analysis. The basic point, however, is to properly see the environment as the originator of what people do, even when this is complex and difficult to observe. He basically was trying to do what Gibson had been doing for perception all along, but for all behaviour.

So, Skinner's answer to the Gestaltists' point that humans engage with bigger units was that *the environments within which we are embedded have more than enough detail and complexity in their consequences and changes to shape human behaviour and its 'bigger units'* and we do not therefore need to resort to 'explanations' of human behaviour that depend upon an internal agent. The main criticisms of Skinner were in the simplistic form of, "I cannot see how behaviour X could be shaped by the environment". The answer is simply, "Well look harder!" And so Skinner embarked upon a career of providing such descriptions of environments that could control behaviour although his later work was unfortunately only conceptual.

Skinner's early research was exemplary for this (Ferster & Skinner, 1957; Skinner, 1935), and clearly demonstrated how changes in nuanced aspects of an organism's environment could change their behaviour in straightforward and replicable ways. (Ironically, almost all research in psychology since Wundt has difficulty with replication, except Gibson's demonstrations, those of the Gestaltists, and Skinner's early experimental research, all of which can be replicated 100 per cent every time. You should think about what this means.)

His later work tried to move into more complex human behaviour (social, language, political) but unfortunately, he did this only conceptually and did not fully explore such environments or contexts through research or learning what had already been shown by the research of sociologists and others (e.g.

Skinner, 1953). What was needed was a full description of all the actual environments and contexts in which humans were shaped, and this actually follows from basic principles of Skinner's work. So, he failed to place human behaviours in the real contexts in which they were shaped—social relationships, economics, politics, patriarchy, culture, discursive communities, etc. This material was always available in sociology, sociolinguistics, and social anthropology but he did not consider those sadly.

Like Gibson then, Skinner began the description of those worlds or environments that shape human seeing (Gibson) and other activities (Skinner). The other books in this series take this further for the more complex human social behaviours, while paying great tribute to the pioneering start by Skinner. The task for *social contextual analysis* is to build on these two monumental achievements but synthesize this with what we also know from the contextual analyses made in sociology, sociolinguistics, and social anthropology.

I will list some of the other radical changes in thinking Skinner gave to us and that I draw upon. As already mentioned, most of these have been watered down, rationalized into traditional use of everyday words, or misunderstood by most writers about psychology. Make sure you read the original versions!

- The subject matter of psychology was not behaviour, nor stimulus and response relations, networks or associations, but was the contingent relations between what an organism does and the external consequences of doing this; what organisms do, how this changes the environment, and how these changes in turn affect the organism.
- What was important was to see how engaging with our environments affected future behaviour; that is, how did the consequence of behaving in a specific environment or context lead to changes in behaviour units? (we will see in Chapter 5 that this is also happening in our 'perceptual systems' but on a very small scale).
- Skinner focused almost exclusively on demonstrating cases when the behaviour led to *more* of that same way of behaving or *less* of that same way of behaving; more complex patterns were less commonly studied, but this was an important start. However, much of what we do changes our worlds but without this leading to either more or less of the same behaviour, instead it leads to new contexts that afford other behaviours altogether; this was noted and named by behaviour analysts but not researched.
- The organism does not need to represent the world; the world contains enough details already to shape nuanced, complex, and creative behaviours.

- There should be less emphasis on theories and hypotheses (cf. Hull) and more on observing and describing what the organisms do in their worlds and what their contexts or environments are like.
- There should be no teleology in learning (a Darwinian model or teleonomy was used) but rather, the behaviours he studied were those *selected by external consequences or changes.*

I will not say more since this book is about continuing this task rather than reviewing all the details of the early research into more simple affordances or contingencies. To understand human behaviour, we must now focus on the 'other' external human contexts that shape what we do—the social, economic, patriarchal, discursive, societal, opportunistic, and cultural. These are mostly difficult to observe—at least with short-term observations—and have been the very cases that made those on Pathway 1 assume that the environment could not contain the answers.

Whatever happened to the 'soul' and the 'mental'? The social and cultural contexts for using language

There is a basic gut feeling, going back to Aristotle, that our experience, consciousness, thinking, mind, or psyche all seem to be different to other parts of our behaviour or actions. This was handled in various ways through the realm of Western philosophy but generally assigned to a vague category of 'the mind' with attempts to reconcile this with the increasingly popular view that ultimately all the answers lay in the human physiology. Descartes was really the first modern philosopher to try and properly reconcile these, but without success, since he (wrongly) claimed that we cannot ever doubt the existence of an experiencing self.

The beginnings of modern psychology, pursuing the study of people by using 'scientific' methods and reasoning, dealt with this in a roundabout way (a linguistic sleight of hand!). Experience seemed different to physiology, but for every human experience a unique set of neural conditions would be found (it was promised). This was called 'psycho-physical parallelism'. Yet, even if we found neural correlates for experiences, they would still be only correlates. This would still not explain why we also have this different world of 'experiencing' such neural correlates. Why would there even be such 'experiences'? Do they have a material basis?

Unfortunately, this is still the state of modern psychology with respect to Aristotle's observations that 'soul' seems different somehow to the other behaviours we do (which I agree with). Despite the further use of verbal sleight of hands and vague words, such as 'epiphenomena', 'emergent properties', 'embodied cognitions', and the like, we are still in the same conceptual framework as Wundt with respect to experience, consciousness, and the mind.

In the next two chapters I will discuss social contextual approaches to *language use* and *thinking* for humans and this will include what has been called the 'soul' or the different 'mental' experiences, and will explain what has been obvious since Aristotle—that these experiences are different to other bodily experiences, *but they still have a material basis*. My solution is that thinking is just the same as using language in conversation and other discourses, but it is not done out loud, and its material basis is how it concretely affects other people. The different 'quality' of soul or consciousness comes about precisely because the thinking is not said out loud and from the contexts that keep them from being said out loud.

These differences between language use said out loud and those not, are what give the soul, the mind, consciousness, or thinking their special experiences that have seemed (wrongly) to be non-material. More importantly, the material parts of our worlds that shape language use, thinking, and why some language is not said out loud, come only from *other people*, but this is hidden and not at all easy to see.

So, catching a ball that is thrown to you is one kind of experience, and saying "please throw me the ball" with someone complying seems different, so the two *seem* to be very different experiences. Moreover, everything about catching a ball we can see, but almost nothing about language use can be seen (*how it changes our external world that then changes what we do next*). What were the contexts for that person to comply with your request and throw you the ball? Do you know?

While in conversation we can sometimes experience that the other person is shaping what we say and do, and vice versa, this is not the case for 'thinking'. So thinking has always *seemed* to have a very different existence, and even a non-material one to people like Aristotle. But the consequences for talking and thinking that come from other people are just as real. They have been just called 'soul' because of these radical differences in how we engage and are shaped by people, compared to catching a ball (Chapters 3 and 4 will describe these external contexts for language use and thinking in more detail).

This was the answer to the Gestaltists' triangle. We respond to the four black lines ("Draw this") and we respond to social contexts to "Say what you see" in a simple fashion to make social life easy. They are both responses to our 'outside' environment, but they appear very different to us, and have since Aristotle, but this is only because they arise from very different contexts. They can occur simultaneously however, which is the source of the 'parallelism'. But the real problem to come, for you, the reader, is that these thoughts, our talking but not out loud, do not even control what we then do. But being in parallel, they give us the strong gut experience that we do what we think and that our thoughts control our behaviour (see Chapter 4 and V5.5 for more detail on this).

Social contextual analysis

Social contextual analysis is not a completely new body of research but a synthesis of what we know about the differences and effects *all* our external environments provide or afford that shape our human behaviours. This includes the work of both Gibson and behaviour analysis but also integrates what we know from sociology, social anthropology, discourse analysis, and sociolinguistics as to how the contexts of social relationships, discursive and societal environments also shape what we do. The latter broadens the sometimes individualistic focus of the first two. Like the Gestalt triangle example from Chapter 1 showed, we cannot just ignore social relationship contexts even when asking people 'what they see'. If we ignore any of these, we will begin to assume that the behaviours arise from an internal source (Pathway 1).

The vision, however, is not to 'borrow' a bit from the other social sciences to build a new psychology. Rather, the vision is to bring them all together as Pathway 2 to form *a united analysis of the material contexts in our worlds that shape what we do*. The divisions between the different disciplines I see as artificial based on obsolete assumptions. To rescue Pathway 2 from the old fork in the road, psychology *needs* to be part of the social sciences (V5), since the real problems of psychology can only be solved by taking seriously the social and societal life contexts that shape what we do.

There are no physiological or 'mental' internal environments of humans that *determine*, *create*, or *originate* what we do. The brain is certainly involved in all we do, but so is the rest of the body. What we do in life is the result of very complex histories of engagement with our environments or contexts. These environments are not just the simple physical environments or 'stimuli' around us, like chairs, cars, food, and buildings, but also our social relationships, cultural contexts, societal worlds, economic worlds, patriarchy, etc. These other contexts are, in fact, also physical environments since in complex ways they shape and determine what we can do and what we do (V5.2). 'Patriarchy' is not just an abstract word but a physical societal system that actually determines much of your behaviour, whether male or female. You have been physically shaped by these systems to behave in certain ways but not others. They are real. You can look at a crowd of men and women and easily see the effects of these societal environments or 'structures' right in front of you (V5.2).

All that these three books are trying to do is to describe in detail the complex environments in which we are immersed, and how they shape what we do. As we have seen in the first chapter, a few psychologists have tried to do this, but it is difficult. Most have given up this task and instead built theories and metaphors (Guerin, 2016b) for 'architectures' of a mind, mental world, processing environment, consciousness, or soul. These are all fictions of language use, although the events they record from observations need to be taken seriously (someone once called the theories of psychology 'interior decoration'). Gibson did this for basic actions of moving around but his 'affordances' of the environment need to include social and societal ones. Skinner tried to do a bigger analysis but did not research social and societal behaviours and so ended up using the simple concepts found in animal research to try and 'explain' more complex aspects of human life, usually in a tautological way.

My simple addition to this (the missing link) is that the more difficult to observe environments that shape what we do are those built upon *social and societal relationships* (whether friends, family or strangers). Hence *social* contextual analysis. In particular, our uses of language also rest completely on social and societal relationships and these are the most difficult to trace how they shape what we do—but they do not originate inside our brains. Luckily, social anthropologists, sociolinguists, and sociologists have been describing these social and societal contexts for many years, and so merging psychology with the other social sciences can help us to replace all those mind, mental, and cognitive 'architectures' (V5). This is what has been missing and forcing otherwise great psychologists to give up looking in the environment for what it is that shapes what we do.

Thorough descriptions of our social, societal, economic, cultural, and patriarchal 'environments', worlds or contexts, are needed to replace the theorizing about any form of 'internal' control of human behaviour. But because these contexts are difficult to observe, especially the external control of language and thinking, we have had a history of trying to study people by metaphorical talk of an internal world (Guerin, 2016b). This is probably the only reason, apart from territorial politics, why we still have a discipline called 'psychology' that is separate from the social sciences.

Sociologists use the term 'sociological imagination' for what I am getting at here. When you see an individual human, you should be able to 'see' *all* the social, societal, cultural, economic, and other contexts that have shaped that person to do what they are doing (Guerin, 2001; Mills, 1959). Historically, psychologists have limited the 'environment' to the objects in the nearby locale. Once we expand this, Pathway 2 can be accomplished easily and with no need to appeal to events 'inside' us.

I will not give an overview of social contextual analysis here for two reasons. First, because it is summarized in part elsewhere (Guerin, 2004, 2016a), and second, because it is not a body of unique facts that can be listed, but a way of approaching thinking and intervention with people (Pathway 2). My previous summaries give an overview of the human contexts of the social, societal, economic, cultural, etc., but they are only a beginning. They also draw on all the social sciences and these all need to be read (V5) and cannot be summarized easily. The basic message, however, is that we need to analyse all the external contexts from which people's behaviours arise to understand why people do, say, and think what they do.

Each person and situation is different but learning to spend time looking for the context is what is important. The catchphrase to respond to criticisms by Pathway 1 psychologies is: "You have not looked hard enough for the contextual originals of people's behaviours, and your methods are not made to do this anyway." From the little bit of history given, the main features of a social contextual approach should be obvious. It is not a new or even "grand theory", but a way of accounting for what humans do (which is why it does not deserve capital letters and an acronym). It integrates what is known from the other social sciences (V5). It is what psychology should have been doing all along, since the 1800s. Here are five features of social contextual analysis:

- The first point of social contextual analysis is to follow Pathway 2; the idea is to explain human behaviours (including talking, thinking, perception, emotion, etc.) by looking at *what it is in the external material world that shapes these.* Human behaviour is shaped and structured by how our worlds are structured, and that is what we must describe. But we need a fully complex version of what external contexts we engage with, this does not mean just the simple objects around us. Social constructionists are correct that everything humans do can be shaped by words, but (1) that is not all that shapes us, and (2) the 'construction' takes place by how the material world is already structured and is not done 'inside' us.

- The second part of the *social* contextual approach acknowledges that everything humans do is partly shaped by their social relationship contexts, unlike worms and bugs. So, all the behavioural engagement with our contexts must be placed in *social and societal contexts.* For humans, the absence of an immediate social context (in the immediate sense of people being present) is only made possible by other social contexts being in place. For example, having money as the major social exchange means that we can do most things without other people being immediately involved. However, this very condition (money) is itself a special *social* condition only made possible by the social properties of capitalism as an economic system. The idea of 'individuals' is fictitious and acting like individuals is only possible anyway through social and societal contexts being in place (Guerin, 2001, V5.5).

- A third part of this approach is that that it applies to all human behaviours, including talking and language use, thinking, perception, emotional behaviours, and 'mental health' behaviours. These behaviours are some of the most difficult to analyse as being shaped by a person's worlds, but it is possible (V6). It is contrary to most psychological approaches but, for example, we can even view thinking as being shaped outside the person and not 'in their head' (see Chapter 4). With these types of behaviours, it is too easy to skip the hard observational work and posit abstract and theoretical constructs that purport to 'explain' what is going on, but have no real basis.

- A fourth part of the social contextual approach is that it changes a lot of notions that are taken for granted in everyday life and that psychology has uncritically accepted (often as its subject matter). It also requires a radical change in research methodologies from those of current psychology, which try to measure samples as points of behaviour that might support abstract theories and models. But if our task is now *to observe and describe over time all the contexts shaping what people do*, we need new research methods. Luckily, the other social sciences have been doing this for a long while.

- And so to the final part of this approach. To understand people by describing all contexts in their worlds that have shaped them, the other social sciences have already been doing this for some time—especially social anthropology, sociology, and sociolinguistics. Not all of these use contextual thinking all the time, but there is a vast amount we can draw upon if we cooperate with them and synthesize. As already mentioned, they also have contextual methodologies that they have been using for a long time. We still need to contextualize what they have found but this should be done anyway. For example, most of the social anthropology research has been done with groups of people living in social and economic contexts every different to Western contexts, so we would not expect to find similar patterns.

We can, in fact, go further with this last point. The very idea that psychology could ignore the other social sciences and yet still claim to be able to 'understand' what humans do without them, only seems at all realistic when (1) you replace careful observing and describing contexts with fictitious theories that everything is being shaped inside an individual's head, (2) you treat these 'internal' processes as *universal* for humans (only the input changes), and (3) you only deal with those parts of life for which the shaping structures of the world are difficult to see. Anything else would look ludicrous from the beginning, but this is what psychology has been built on.

A brief overview of social contextual analysis

The point so far is that to analyse people's actions (these already include perception), talking, and thinking, we must do careful observations and analyses of all their contexts. Psychologists have largely ignored the way our societal and cultural contexts have a huge impact on shaping what we do, and have tried instead to suggest that our decisions are made internally. But sociology, social anthropology, and sociolinguistics can supply these analyses, because they have been doing that for longer than psychology has even existed (V5 will show better how we can, and need to, join forces in an a-disciplinary vision).

Some of the main social behaviour categories of what humans do with each other are as follows:

> compete, cooperate, bond, bully, manage a self-image, share, agree, distance, reciprocate, hedge, protect, complain, control, support, conflict, give, take, apologize, be polite, be rude, be humorous, tell or act out stories, induce positive and negative emotions, show off, be humble.

These are the sorts of things (in everyday words) we do with each other while pursuing our lives—in fact, *in order to pursue our lives.* Sometimes we use these for our own selfish outcomes, sometimes we do them for the benefit of both parties involved, and sometimes we might do these just to help someone else and it might look like we get nothing out of the social behaviour at all. We also have many different ways of doing each of these. The next chapter will show how we do most of these quicker and more efficiently using language (whether for good or bad).

What are resources?

A good exercise at this point is to think of all your different social relationships (including the people at the supermarket) and what resources are involved. Include both what they get through you and what you get through them.

Resources can be any of the things we try to get in life to make our lives work: a job, money, love, attention, food, water, shelter, pleasure, laughter, etc. (Guerin, 2016a). The list can go on and on but is not really that important to us. You cannot analyse much merely by knowing the resources people are after—since you do not know the context for them. In modern society, everyone is after money so that does not help us. Nor can you understand people by thinking there is a 'basic' list of needs or requirements—typically food, water, shelter, sex, company. This is like knowing the molecular structure of wood (cellulose primarily) and thinking that you now can construct a table or carve a large wooden sculpture.

It is far more useful to analyse people's resources *in context*, which means looking at 'resource–social relationship pathways' instead. But there are some useful tricks to thinking about the 'resources' people seem to want or pursue in any situation:

- What things or events are people working for or putting energy into obtaining?
- What do people gain from this situation?
- What are the interests here or what might be at stake here?
- What do people say they want?
- Most resources involve *access to further resources* as the outcomes rather than tangible and edible objects such as food.
- *Escaping or avoiding bad things* is a powerful resource but difficult to analyse in reality because we do not see tangible outcomes when successful.

So, we need to find out what people seem to be after when doing their social behaviours and even what they say they are after (Guerin, 2016a). But this is not simple because understanding always depends upon knowing the contexts better. Knowing that people want or need food as a resource does not help us much. For one person this means only cordon bleu food while for another it means just basic bread and cheese with some fruit. Only the context or 'natural ecology' of the person will help us understand the difference, and these contexts are primarily the person's *social relationships*, but also their economic context, opportunities, culture, history, etc.

What are resource–social relationship pathways?

What exactly do humans do with all these social behaviours, resources, and contexts? There are different ways of talking about this question, but I am going to use the idea of *resource–social relationship pathways*. I like to use this term because it makes explicit a few important points:

- In life we all pursue the resources we need but these depend upon our life contexts (for example, what opportunities we first have where we are born).

- All our resources come through social relationships so we cannot disentangle the two, and culture is just a historical form of this.
- Even getting resources through strangers is a form of social relationship with special properties.
- There are several types of resources with different properties and they therefore need different social behaviours and pathways to obtain them.
- We do not mercilessly and ruthlessly pursue resources and try and compete or beat others for them, since human history suggests that cooperating or sharing with other people is probably the best way of getting resources (with forms of bullying not far behind, sadly).
- Many of the resources we 'need' or try to obtain we do not really need except that they help our relationships stay together so we can cooperate, and this is vitally important.
- In V6.6 I will argue that what I call the resource–social relationship pathways are the same as what Marx called the *social relations of production.*

For example, in modern Western society you can use apples to get money and you can use money to get apples, but each of these will work through very different resource–social relationship pathways. But just analysing social relationships and just analysing resources is not enough. We need to know *in context* what resources people are pursuing and exchanging and through what social relationships. Someone in a context of economic wealth can pursue different pathways than someone who is poor. Most females are still widely constrained by the societal contexts we call patriarchy and often have restricted opportunities in both resources and the social relationships they can pursue.

The conclusion is that if you really want to understand someone, or do a biography, you need to observe the contexts in which they pursue resources through social relationships and the contexts that made them possible. And indeed, if you really want to understand *yourself*, or do an *auto*biography, you need to observe the contexts in which you have pursued resources through social relationships and the contexts that made them possible.

The point is that if two people are speaking then you will not understand why they are talking and why they are using the language they do until you know the resource–social relationship pathways. And these pathways are shaped externally, they do not originate from inside us. This is a broader vision for discourse analysis than looking for 'what is at stake' in conversations, although along the same track.

Where to next?

Having briefly introduced how we can understand (analyse) people's general behaviours without resorting to abstract 'internal' events, I can mostly refer you to such analyses in sociology, sociolinguistics, and social anthropology, as well as examples from psychology mentioned earlier (put together in Guerin, 2004, 2016a). You can begin tracing people's resource–social relationship pathways and what their opportunities in life were that resulted in them, and how they manage these.

My summary of human contexts (there are other ways to do this), are to consider in detail the following contexts:

- Our social relationships (including stranger relationships).
- The economic systems we live in and how these affect us.
- Cultural practices of smaller groups.
- The opportunities afforded or stratified by various ossified societal structures (race, class, wealth, oppression, etc.).
- The contexts of colonization and how those shape the colonized, the colonizers, and the descendants of both.
- Patriarchal systems of shaping differential behaviours.
- How the above have formed and changed through historical periods.

Much of this material comes from the social sciences (V5). The point for psychologists is that it is all *necessary* for understanding any behaviour of humans—it is not optional.

But there are a few difficult cases that require more detail up front, as they are difficult for both psychologists and the other social sciences. These are the behaviours that have commonly been assumed for centuries to originate from within us, and that have fuelled the fires of Pathway 1:

- language;
- thinking;
- perceiving;
- emotion.

They will be dealt with in turn in the next chapters.

References

Bruner, J. (1973). *Beyond the information given: Studies in the psychology of knowing.* New York, NY: W. W. Norton & Company.
Deleuze, G. (1994). *Difference and repetition.* New York, NY: Columbia University Press.

Ferster, C. B., & Skinner, B. F. (1957). *Schedules of reinforcement.* New York, NY: Appleton-Century-Crofts.

Gibson, J. J., & Gibson, E J. (1955). Perceptual learning: Differentiation or enrichment? *Psychological Review, 62,* 32–41.

Guerin, B. (2001). Individuals as social relationships: 18 ways that acting alone can be thought of as social behavior. *Review of General Psychology, 5,* 406–428.

Guerin, B. (2004). *Handbook for analyzing the social strategies of everyday life.* Reno, NV: Context Press.

Guerin, B. (2016a). *How to rethink human behavior: A practical guide to social contextual analysis.* London: Routledge.

Guerin, B. (2016b). *How to rethink psychology: New metaphors for understanding people and their behavior.* London: Routledge.

Mills, C. W. (1959). *The sociological imagination.* Oxford: Oxford University Press.

Skinner, B. F. (1935). The generic nature of the concepts of stimulus and response. *Journal of General Psychology, 12,* 40–65.

Skinner, B. F. (1953). *Science and human behavior.* New York, NY: Free Press.

3 Language is a socially transitive verb—huh?

How can language possibly arise from our environments?

Language must surely be one of the weirdest things in the universe, and it has caused much pain for those trying to figure out where it comes from and how it works. One of the main reasons for this pain, however, is that people usually assume wrong ideas about what it is there for in the first place. And so they end up in agony trying to figure out how it does what they think it does, when it doesn't.

As mentioned in Chapter 1, our everyday words and explanations usually mess us up because they are shorthand strategies and easy solutions to keep a social peace among people. And everything that tries to 'talk about language itself' has really messed us up as well, including about 300 years of Western philosophy.

In terms of the goals of this book and pursuing Pathway 2, therefore, language and thinking (they are really the same as we will see) are the most unlikely candidates for me showing you how all behaviour can arise from our external worlds rather than from 'within' us (along with perception and emotion). While we certainly talk about our worlds a lot, language and thinking are notoriously placed in everyday lingo as arising from within us. 'We' speak and 'we' think, and both arise from this mysterious 'within us' space. Descartes even famously declared that we only know we exist at all because we think, and that we cannot doubt this!

Here are some of the main culprits for mis-thinking language. When someone says something in everyday conversation, the focus is usually on:

- What was the person trying to *express*?
- What was the person trying to *communicate*?
- What was the person trying to *refer to*?
- What was the person trying to *represent*?
- What did the person *really mean?*

The first and second also run riot when analysing literature or music. The next two have properly messed up 300 years of Western philosophy and (later) psychology, and occasionally those talking about music also try to use these to make sense of music. And the last is a general and widespread problem for understanding language use. They all lead us to 'inner' determinants of speaking (and thinking), traipsing down Pathway 1.

Once again, as we saw in Chapter 2, these numerous (misguided) ways to talk arise because it seems as if we cannot 'see' any environment that could possibly lead to talking and thinking. While I might believe that seeing a cat 'triggers' my saying "Cat!" or "There is a cat", what about when we talk about pink unicorns or my deceased uncle? Plato even invented an otherworldly 'environment' of ideas or concepts to which these refer.

Instead of using these ways of talking (dump them for serious study, but keep them for everyday conversations), we need to ponder the role of all the environments for language use through three questions:

- How much is language use part of our lives and worlds?
- How do our uses of language arise from the world?
- What does language do in the external world that then has real consequences?

What I want to demonstrate for you is that *language does arise solely from our external worlds* but not in the places where people have been looking. Seeing a cat does not 'trigger' my saying "There is a cat!"; rather, people and my real, material, but complex social contexts do this. And this is all observable in principle (although often difficult in practice). Try thinking this way—if you see a cat there is no 'point' (effect) for you then to say, "There is a cat!" unless another person might hear it. What would 'trigger' me to say instead, "There is a cat's tail!" when I see a cat? Only if it were socially relevant (or afforded, as Gibson would say).

But before getting to those three big questions above, I first need to orient you to this total reboot of how we talk about language. How to get you turning explanations of language use inside out!

What you most need to know about language use

In the last chapter I gave a list of some things we commonly do with other people, even when they are not present. We can do all these without words but this is usually less efficient, slower, and with more mistakes. Think about all your social interactions with anybody at all in the last week, and see if you can roughly classify them in these sorts of ways:

You and the supermarket people *cooperated* and they *trusted* you (although security was *monitoring* you nearby) as they *gave* you some fruit and vegetables (which you had selected) and you *reciprocated* by *giving* them money. You *apologized* to your Mother *politely* for not *visiting* earlier and then you *gave* her some flowers and you both *chatted* and mostly *agreed* while *discussing* some things (you might have been *polite* and *agreed* even when you would have *argued* and had *conflicts* with friends over the same issues). Someone at work tried to *get the agreement* of the others to *cooperate* with something you *disagreed* with, so you *made a speech* and *exhorted them* (a small form of *bullying*) *not to go along* with it because of the bad consequences you then *outlined*.

So, what have these social behaviours got to do with language use? Why start with social behaviours and not language? Box 3.1 outlines the starting point and the final punchline for the whole chapter.

Box 3.1 The purpose or use of language is not to talk

The purpose or use of language is doing our social behaviours—to change what other people do as we pursue our resource–social relationship pathways alongside the many other ways we do social behaviours that do *not* involve language. And with that, all the mysteries of psychology and philosophy disappear.

The first lines in Box 3.1 might seem possible, but the last sentence probably seems all wrong. Solving all the mysteries of psychology and philosophy by rethinking language? Solve all the issues of consciousness, unconsciousness, the mind, thinking, etc.? But I will show later that the problems in psychology and philosophy have arisen exactly because of misguided views of language and how it works (Guerin 2016b). It is only when you treat *language as one unique way humans do their social behaviours*, and focus on the external, material *social* consequences from speaking and writing (and thinking), that you can get somewhere with these mysteries.

For centuries, language has been believed to have magic powers, at least some forms of it. The hypnotist could speak their special words and a person would fall into a trance! Children seemed to learn language so quickly that mysterious powers were assigned to our DNA to give us a 'hard-wire capacity' for language (Pathway 1 logic). Others dreamed that a public health campaign could list the serious health risks of cigarettes and (supposedly) people would read these words and immediately stop smoking. Some people while awake can hear voices that sound like there are real persons talking nearby, but they are taken to have either the mysterious powers of the shaman or else a disease in the brain labelled psychosis.

I am going to front up to language, confront its so-called magic powers, and instead find the answers in its *natural social ecology*. The natural ecology of language is in our social relationships or contexts— other people! That is where these 'mysterious' powers come from, not from the words themselves. If our social relationships have no reciprocity or power, then our words stop working as social behaviour. The problems have occurred when psychologists and philosophers have taken language out of its natural social ecology of social relationships and resources and looked for the answers in either the words themselves or inside our body (cf. V5.1).

This chapter *is* about language, but with so much more than that usually implies once we put language in its rightful ecology—as a special way in which we do all the social behaviours we do anyway. When analysing language use you need to frame it as: *what is this language 'trying' to accomplish as social behaviour, and with whom?* I am going to explain language in this novel way.

What is language?

The trick now is that language is just *one* way to do all these social behaviours to pursue our resource–social relationship pathways in life, although it does have special properties that I will go through carefully later. In the Western world at least, it is probably the most common way for us to do all of our social behaviours. We talk more than we do anything else, but it gets us what we need! So with this crazy system of saying or writing a limited set of words made up out of a limited set of letters, we can do all those social behaviours listed earlier, without breaking into a sweat. But there are a lot of pre-conditions or contexts required for this system to work and get things done. But when it does work, and is speeded up by using grammar and other regularities, it is an amazingly powerful social system.

But we always have to remember that *words by themselves do not have any power to make people do anything*. I can say "Give me a million dollars" to my cat or even to a billionaire, and there will not be any effect just by saying this. It is the *contexts for our social behaviours* that have this power, the resource exchanges that are consequences of the social relationships involved. The hypnotist's words do not have any effect by themselves, otherwise I could just read out those words and it would affect anyone listening (and it would actually affect me too as I read them, if that is all that was needed). Rather it is the social and historical contexts arranged by the hypnotist that do all the work.

This is indeed a strange position on language you are reading, where I confess that language is not primarily about talking and that we cannot do anything just with words alone even though it is one of our most frequent behaviours. However, if we think of it as just one more way to do our social behaviours and get the things we need in life, it makes more sense—we need to analyse the whole context. And using language is so very important because it is one of the most economical, easy, efficient, and certainly widespread ways of getting resources through resource-social... relationship pathways and conducting our lives. And we will see it has many unusual social properties that make it extremely valuable to humans as well as perilous (see Chapter 7)! (The only problem is that it takes up a lot of our early life to learn how to use words for very nuanced social effects.)

Why language is a socially transitive verb

Calling language use a socially transitive verb is another way to remember that by itself language is a pretty useless behaviour that we do a lot. A transitive verb is a 'doing word' that requires an object in the sentence. "I hit" is strange because it needs an object—"I hit the kerb", "I hit into thin air". "Hit" is a transitive verb. On the other hand, "I arrived" does not need an object (although you might typically provide a place), and is called intransitive.

What I am getting you to remember by repeating 'language use is a socially transitive verb' ad nauseum is that (1) language always requires an object for it do anything (like 'hitting' does), and (2) that these objects must be social—another human who speaks the same language. Language by itself does nothing; language said to a chair does nothing, and language said to a person who has no training in your specific language also does nothing. They are wasted efforts.

Here is the bottom-line mantra for language:

> Language use does things to people
> and that is *all* it does and *only* to people.

That is, language is a doing word, a verb, and it always does things to something, and that something is always other people. We should be able to say: "I languaged you" but not "I languaged". We do say the former but in more specific forms: "I asked you", "I persuaded you", "I pleaded with you". Saying just, "I asked", "I persuaded", or "I pleaded" do not make sense without more social context.

To spell out a little more detail, language use only does things to people *who have been trained in the same language.* Not just anybody. So, the proper question for any type of language use is: *what is this doing to people and what has it done in the past that changes the speaker's world?* Let me drive this home to you. Think about each of these and the different accomplishments of each:

Telling a story to a friend:

What is this doing to people and what has it done in the past that changes the speaker's world?

Telling the same story to a stranger on a bus:

What is this doing to people and what has it done in the past that changes the speaker's world?

Telling gossip:

What is this doing to people and what has it done in the past that changes the speaker's world?

Asking someone to help you move a desk:

What is this doing to people and what has it done in the past that changes the speaker's world?

Saying a simple "Hello!" to a person in your office in the morning:

What is this doing to people and what has it done in the past that changes the speaker's world?

Telling a joke to your siblings:

What is this doing to people and what has it done in the past that changes the speaker's world?

Speaking in poetry rather than prose to an audience:

What is this doing to people and what has it done in the past that changes the speaker's world? What is poetry doing differently to prose?

(Guerin, 2020)

How much is language use part of our lives and worlds?

Language use is probably the most frequent thing we do in this world. We completely *overlearn* language use, which is what happens when you learn a skill and then keep on learning it more and more. Practising over and over, going beyond 100 per cent.

This overlearning will become very important in the next chapter on thinking. We learn to say things in contexts and then we overlearn these. Every time we are in those contexts, we will have *all* those many language responses (although we can only say one of them out loud at a time—and this is one way that thinking arises). As adults, we end up having several language responses in almost every and any context in our lives. Even in brand new contexts we might not know what we can *do* but we can certainly *talk* about it!

For example, suppose I presented you suddenly with a hurdy-gurdy, which hopefully you have never seen before or perhaps not even heard of (look them up). You might try *doing* one or two things with it, such as turning the handle gently, or touching the strings. But you would not be short of things to *say*—even if you did not know what this strange thing was! You can describe what it looks like, describe what you think it might be, tell your story about the last time you were given a strange musical instrument, discuss why I am showing this to you, mention that you like listening to music but are not good at performing, talk about the old LP recording your father owned of hurdy-gurdy music, or even go off on a tangent talking about Donovan. There is almost no end to the language responses we can make.

The important point here is that we have a huge repertoire of language responding; we are never short of words, and in most situations, there are *several* things we can say. But we also must remember that all this language responding arises *from the world* and is not 'inside us' (Pathway 2), even once we have learned the responses thoroughly. Our contexts or fields are broad rather than just 'stimuli' (see Chapter 1) and likewise our 'perceptions' of the world are context-driven actions not passive reception and representations (see Chapter 5).

How do our uses of language arise from the world?

Instead of assuming that our uses of language arise from within us, are stored in a 'memory' or are even hard-wired (all theoretical metaphors), we need to look harder at the (social) environment to get the answers. That is the battle cry of this book remember. *Viva la* Pathway 2! So where in the world do we get our languages?

Consider the following:

- แมวอยู่บนเสื่อ
- η γάτα είναι στο χαλί
- 고양이 매트에는
- мачку је на подлогу
- القط على حصيرة

Presuming you do not know these written languages, we would normally say in everyday conversation that you do not know what they mean, or what they express, communicate, represent, or refer to. In this book, as you should know by now, the real problem we have is that *we do not know what to do* when we see these. We have no external context for responding (training) in a way that is 'appropriate' to get something done, at least to a speaker of these languages.

(Of course, as I emphasized in the previous section, we would still not be *short* of things to say in our own language, even if we have no social context for doing social behaviour with these languages: "Oh, doesn't that writing look pretty!"; "I was never good at languages as a child, I even failed French"; "Aren't they some kind of language?"; "I think the fourth one might be Russian"; "They are probably all swear words!")

But you also need to remember that there are millions of people on this planet who can look at those sentences above and know what to *do* 'appropriately' when they appear in different contexts. How are they so wise? And that gives us the clue: clearly, we need to find a speaker or a community of speakers and learn what to do with those sentences and when to use them appropriately.

My question, therefore, is, *how would you actually find out what to do 'appropriately'* when you read these? Obviously, a stock answer is that you would need to learn these five languages, but what does that actually mean? Do you think you could learn these by looking at cats, for example (a clue; they are all about cats)? If the meanings of these words are something about cats, could we learn them by observing cats? Would looking long and hard at Korean cats help you at all with the third one? Will we get a clue observing Arabic cats, perhaps for the last one? Clearly not, and the point I want to get across that that *our words do not actually arise from those parts of our environments and worlds.* You are looking in the wrong place. This is the problem that centuries of Western philosophy has had— thinking that the 'truth' of language is about what it *refers* to correctly or not. Language does not 'refer to things', but it might refer other people to 'things' in the right contexts.

The material basis or embodiment of using language is not in the words or objects but in the effects of our social behaviours with other people. We need to realize that words and sentences do not arise from the world itself. I can never learn the English word 'cat' from looking at or interacting with an English cat, or the Persian word for 'cat' by looking at a Persian cat. We only get the words from speakers of a language training us what to do. I can only learn them from speakers in a community. We have to look to the environment, as this whole book is doing, the 'meaning' or referent is not the place to look, but that is what both common sense and Western philosophy have mistakenly done for a long time.

In summary:

- Our effects of languages, sentences, and words arise from our environments not from our heads (Pathway 2), but they only arise from our *social* environments—from people and their consequences.
- All that our languages, sentences, and words can accomplish in this world is to change the behaviour of people, they never change other objects (how they accomplish this is the topic for the next section).

There are some other important points we can learn from all this so far:

- The words and symbols are arbitrary. I have elsewhere described language as the first ever virtual reality (Guerin, 2016b), and also as the original matrix (Guerin, 2017).
- There must be a community of people who agree (socially cooperate) to act in the same way for all their words (but poets and liars know how to take advantage of this).
- *The community must sustain itself in order to sustain the language*, and this already requires a number of social and political conditions to be in place.
- So our language use is already steeped in social and political contexts and constraints.
- The 'power' to make words actually have effects on other people therefore depends on the social and political relationships between people, not on the meaning or anything else about the words; the words themselves cannot do anything to listeners.
- The language must be useful or functional for people to keep using it—it must be able to *do things in the world* (the next topic) and be functional for it to be maintained.
- Because all this is functional only through people, *the only thing languages can ever do is to change what people do* (the words 'cat' and 'chat' cannot do anything to a cat—try it out).

It is important for you to get a real feel for these points, as the main problems and issues with psychology and Western philosophy arise here. Most scholars have assumed that 'words refer to things' and so philosophers look to find a 'connection' in the world between, say, the word 'cats' and cats. These 'connections' might be epistemological theories for philosophers and 'neural networks' for psychologists.

Other philosophical issues that arise from wrongly conceiving language are: can we say with certainty that the statement 'all cats have four legs' is true? How do we support this as certain knowledge? How can we prove this is true, especially when it actually refers to *all* the cats in the universe? And what about 'all unicorns are pink'? What is that referring to? Can that be true?

It is from reasoning and explanations like this that Western philosophers have also resorted to inventing 'internal' and fictitious worlds just like Pathway 1 psychologists. Our words seemingly refer to a concept inside us that then refers to the outside world or to a Platonic world of ideas. Psychologists have followed in the same way. There must be a connection between the word 'cats' and real cats so they have invented memory storage areas in the head, neuronal networks from cat to 'cat', 'prototypes' of cats in the cognitive architecture, behavioural associations that are 'stamped in' and probable reside somewhere in our brains, reflex arcs between seeing a cat and making the noise 'cat', and so on (see Chapter 1).

Very few have pinpointed that saying 'cat' is shaped by people *only*, and *never* by cats. Cats shape us to pat, look, feed them, and much more, but cats do not shape the actual talk that is done about cats—that is only developed between their *hoomans*. But some philosophers, psychologists, and sociologists have come close to these views. While each has problems, I believe, some of the ideas given here have been shaped by Wittgenstein, Skinner, Vygotsky, Kantor, Bentley, and others.

> In the long term language is more dependent on the social world than the other way around. It is true that linguistic interchange facilitates social intercourse, and that language can be used to create structures of understanding that define and redefine the world for speakers. Despite the reasonableness of this view, however, the world, in a pinch, turns out to be able to force its reality on language. Language does facilitate social intercourse, but if the social situation is sufficiently compelling, language will bend.
>
> (Sankoff, 1980, p. xxi)

So for our voyage along the newly opened up Pathway 2, language use (and thinking in the next chapter) certainly arises from the external world, but specifically from the material world of discursive people cooperating (although they can use the words then to *not* cooperate or to fight). This is both because people have to train you in the language and because getting words to do thing requires some 'power' (social reciprocity, exchanges) in your social relationships.

What does language do in the world that has consequences?

So far, I have tried to show that language arises from our external world but only from social consequences shaped by people, not from the things we are 'talking about'. The question to ask is not "What do these words mean?" but "What do I get people to do with these words and in what social contexts does that even work?"

Humans have developed these cooperative systems we call languages in which people learn to do things to arbitrary written words and sounds, and we greatly overlearn them. These two features bring about some amazing changes in how humans work, changes that have led to Western philosophy, fictional writing, inventions, and other fictional wonders. For centuries intellectuals and laypeople have been treating language use and thinking as special parts of the universe, as if they existed in another dimension, spirit world, soul, or internal mental realm.

The purported differences between word and non-word actions, how-ever, come from the differences in their very material and down-to-earth contextual and consequential properties. For example, in everyday life I cannot jump 20 metres into the air unassisted. I cannot do that with my body and the world of gravity. However, I can easily *talk about* jumping 20 metres into the air unassisted because *the material consequences of my words come from the people* listening and responding to my talk (such as laughing with me or at me), and *not* from my body, gravity, or the muscles in my legs. Both are determined by external, worldly material effects, but very different ones!

Because words only affect the people in our worlds, this means that we can talk about almost anything and still get some (social) effects occurring or a change of (social) context—some consequences. *What we say does not even have to be true, it just has to change the social context and it becomes consequential.* I can say, "I am the reincarnation of Genghis Khan" (which is not true by the way) and still get some consequences from others. This could be laughing and a new view of me as a funny guy, or they might try to get me locked up. Either way, without expending much energy I can have an effect in the social world (this is also one reason why so many of the so-called 'mental health disorders' are about language and thinking, see V6). What this means then, is:

Words and language uses do not have properties at all of either truth or falsity.

Words can be neither true nor false; they are events that can do things to people and have consequences from people given the right contexts.

Nothing more.

Another powerful property of language use is that we can change our contexts without using our body by getting someone else to do this. Instead of getting up from where I am sitting and putting on the kettle to boil, I can yell out over a distance, "Can you please put the kettle on for me?" I can even have effects over time if the social relationship is right, "Can you please put the kettle on for me in ten minutes?"

For this to actually work, materially work, it relies on a great number of social conditions being in place, but we can manage this given the right circumstances (if the person in the kitchen is angry at you, there will be no boiled water). We can also do this over distance and time as well. These are effects we can have on the environment that animals cannot do, nor people without a language. Notice also that we cannot do this with a person who has not been trained in our same language for 15–20 years. We keep forgetting that pre-condition, until we work with such people (maybe an immigrant who does not yet know your language) and have to try and 'communicate' with them. This simply means that we try to get them to do things but without our language system working; a bit like putting a nail in the wall when you do not have a hammer.

As also pointed out earlier, language means that even while we are doing things with our body, such as lifting, during perceptual responding, or driving a car, we can be having multiple, concurrent language responding occurring, although we will see in what follows that we can still only *say* one thing out loud at a time.

One other reason we have *multiple* language responses is that we have many different audiences with different social consequences for what is said. This also has the property that we can easily say *contradictory* things because different audiences produce different changes in context when we say the same things. What we say becomes constrained by our audiences, but different audiences mean that we can still have a wide range of multiple language responses. Thoughts can be contradictory in the same way that we can talk about things that are not true. This is not the case for non-word responding—we cannot pick up a vase and not pick up a vase at the same time. We can, however, tell one audience that we picked up the vase and tell another audience that we did not.

Summarizing the general properties of language use

This sort of *natural social ecology view of language use in social behaviour* has been built through a number of rebels who fought (academically) against the typical views of what language is and how it works. I have adapted and changed all of these, but my predecessors from whom I have learned much, even where I disagree, include: Wittgenstein, Vygotsky, Skinner, A. F. Bentley, Deleuze, Bakhtin, Austin, Vološinov, Hymes, Burke, Ryle, Kantor, Eckert, Berk, Coward and Ellis, Hekman, Rorty, Sapir, Bloomfield, Chomsky, Hjelmslev, Pike, Saussure, Jakobson, Whorf, Morris, Firth, and Halliday.

To summarize, the main claims in the Pathway 2 language approach (Guerin, 2003b, 2004, 2016a) are as follows:

- Language use is maintained only by affecting people—it can do nothing to anything else in the universe to sustain it.
- Language use only affects people if they are also trained in your language, but such training takes a long time and is hidden or forgotten about as a precondition (a social context) afterwards (hence we stick it inside the head).
- The power of language to get things done only comes from material resources that are organized through (and are consequences of) talking to people, from our social relationships; nothing comes from the words themselves.
- As opposed to all Western philosophy, the properties of true and false therefore do not apply to *any* uses of language; they have an effect in our engagement with the social environments or they do not.
- Language use is one way of accomplishing all the social behaviours we need to do in life to get our resources, and these outcomes are where language gets its power to do things—words by themselves without any social reciprocity are just hot air.
- Because language use is materially based in practical social outcomes, and *not* in what is talked about, we can therefore talk about anything—even imaginary things—and still get real material outcomes (from whatever listeners do).
- Humans are very social and need constant organizing of relationships, and so they talk a lot, about anything and everything, including things that do not need talking about and things that do not exist otherwise.
- Talk in different types of social relationships will therefore differ, such as talk between people in kin-based communities and stranger-based communities (Western societies).

- Thinking and consciousness are just normal discourses but not said out loud, and they are *not* 'talking to yourself' (more in the next chapter— 'the audience for thinking is not the thinker').

For language use analyses (discourse analysis, conversational analysis, social contextual analysis, sociolinguistics), therefore, we need to observe and document the following:

- What do the different uses of language do to people and how do they respond?
- In what social contexts does language use do different things to people?
- What outcomes or changes from the listeners or readers then affect the speaker or writer into the future?
- How do these fit into the people's resource–social relationship pathways?

So, we cannot do discourse analysis by just analysing the words used and word strategies. As most versions of discourse analysis state (see reference list at the end of the chapter), we must always observe and analyse the following:

- The social and societal context of the people involved, including the resource–social relationship pathways for these people, i.e. what are they trying to accomplish (social analysis, SA; see summaries in Guerin, 2016a).
- The language used and the language strategies used (language analysis, LA; see summaries in the discourse analysis books in the references).

Discourse analysis (DA) then puts these together to show how the language strategies get people to do various behaviours for the resource–social relationship pathways in those relationships:

SA + LA = DA

Some tricks for analysis are as follows:

- The material outcomes for language use are only ever *changes in the social behaviour of other people*, not the production or distribution of resources more directly (unless you think talking to vegetables helps them grow: "Call any vegetable!").

- We can rarely observe these effects of language use directly since most of what is going on comes from the social relationship histories,
- This means that the 'power' of causing changes when using language and 'thinking' has usually been attributed to something else—typically brain processes, 'cultural' processes, mental processes, the mind, 'cognitive information processing, magic, the soul, the gods or spirits, or charisma.
- But the 'power' for words to affect people comes *externally*, from what people do depending upon our histories of exchange.

Here are some other mantras (or conclusions) to take away from this and see whether you can make sense of them in your life:

- The words that are said are perhaps the smallest or least important part of what is going on when two people talk. The social contexts for social behaviour outcomes are of key importance; I might have tried other strategies to accomplish something before the language strategy you observe, telling you a joke is not about telling you a joke, but about changing our past and future social relationship.
- The material basis or concrete nature of language are the social contexts in which the speaker and listener are immersed, not the words or anything 'mental'.
- What makes language do anything are not the words but the total external contexts *that usually cannot be seen at that moment.*
- If saying to someone "Please pass the salt" actually works and they do it, this is *not* about anything to do with the words themselves but the history of the social relationship and exchanges of resources in that social relationship.
- Words used without a social context have no 'magical power' to do anything; you might as well talk to a tree.
- Social relationships come before the language use.

The problem is that in a few hundred years of trying to explain language use, people have been trying to explain the wrong thing!

What is wrong with the other views of language use?

When you look at books on language, they are similar in many ways. The linguistics ones go for 'linguistic structures' as the basis for language to work, and the psychology ones go for 'processing information' and 'internal structures' or 'cognitive architectures' to *originate* speaking and writing (V5.2). These often have the following issues:

- They are vague on how to explain thinking.
- Most spend a long time on grammar as if it were key.
- The social analyses are usually crude, such as only using social class as the unit of social relationship.
- They tend to be pretty unanimous both that language happens in the brain and that parts of the production of language are hard-wired into our DNA and history.

You might have guessed that I am against all these ways of thinking about language, but, in fact, I do not disagree with everything, I just dispute their focus and the importance they attach to it. Learning about how words are pronounced and how different social groups, even within a language, pronounce them in different ways, is important. And grammatical structures are important and deserves attention (V5.2). But these alone do not tell us why people are talking at all, with whatever accent, and with whatever grammar. However, there is also good sociolinguistic research looking at the social and political contexts for accents developing and disappearing that fills some of this. Later in this chapter I will try to focus on the functions of the different 'structures' and then we can look at it in more detail.

How should we analyse conversations and other discourses?

There are many ways to do discourse analysis, but they differ in nuanced ways. They all try to analyse what pieces of discourse are doing within their social and political contexts, but in many (most?) cases, the social analysis is weak or cursory. With Pathway 2 we can now think more clearly about these issues. As already mentioned, DA for me is about doing an analysis of the linguistic features or strategies (LA), and a social analysis of all the contexts (SA): SA + LA = DA (see Box 3.2).

This puts the analysis in the correct material world, of social behaviour and its outcomes, rather than in the head, neurons, or the mind.

What makes language work at all are *all of the contexts of that talk and preceding that talk*, including the history of those persons, the social exchanges they have had and how this had shaped their behaviours, all the discourses they have been immersed in from other relationships, their communities and the societies that shape so many of our discourses that we then perform individually, their cooperation and conflicts over resources in the past, etc.

Box 3.2 An example of analysing language use (SALADA)

Notice the first sentence of the last paragraph in the previous section. Read the whole sentence again here: "You might have guessed that I am against all these ways of thinking about language, but, in fact, I do not disagree with everything, I just dispute their focus and the importance they attach to it."

For the LA we could analyse my double negative and the grammar I used, and we could certainly categorize the linguistics features such as the use of the limp word 'dispute' and the passive tone with commas. There was a lot of writing 'as if factual' (Guerin, 2016a), such as 'but', 'in fact', 'I just', and also uses of 'categorization' in 'their focus' and 'they attach'.

But, for the analysis of this book, what is really, really important in analysing this sentence is analysing what this sentence is doing *socially, in context* (SA), what is this sentence doing to my readers and how am I hedging the worst outcomes? What is this doing to social behaviour?

Roughly, the SA is: I am about to disagree with almost all previous writers on language, but I really, really want to do this in a socially acceptable way. And in this case, you, the readers, are my main social context. I want you to keep reading and not have you stop because I am criticizing your favourite writers on language or I appear arrogant. I am trying to keep you on my side by telling you that I can see what these famous writers were getting at, and that I merely want to change their focus rather than throw them all completely out the door!

That is all very nice, but in a more cynical social analysis, I might not care so much about *you* but really want to sell the book and also get fame and fortune from my peers and employers. Whichever, the important point of this digression is that what I wrote, and I could have written it several different ways, was about my *social goals* with my readers (if there are any!) and other people in my life, but analysing *just* the grammar and morphology do not much help for this. And my resources gained in this example of a resource–social relationship pathway? It could be money, fame, teaching you a better view of language, appearing as a nice person, etc.

So, DA would link the way I wrote what I did (LA) with my social and other (economic) contexts (SA), trying to analyse what my uses of language were trying to do to listeners, even when they did not work (my resource–social relationship pathways).

If I had different resource–social relationship pathways I could have tried a much bolder version (LA) of that sentence, which might have put some of you off reading any further (SA), but impressed others of you (SA) to read and buy more of my books, by my audacity and promise that I have all the answers. To do this strategy, for example, I could have written instead:

One conclusion I have come to after decades of researching and observing language use, is that every single previous writer has got it wrong! They have all made totally unsubstantiated assumptions that have led them to what I will show to be completely absurd theories and conjectures! It is almost an historical conspiracy! But you will find out, in this book only, how to do accurate analysis of language use and not make their mistakes.

In fact, I would probably sell more books writing like this, but my peers would not be impressed. This is a resource–social relationship pathway conflict for me. Sadly, I need to keep my day job, although it would be more fun to write in a pop-psychology style as if I had all the answers!

To reiterate:

- The words said are perhaps the smallest or least important part of what is going on when two people talk.
- The material basis or concrete nature of language are the contexts in which the speaker and listener are immersed, not the words or anything 'mental' (which is why we need to know the resource–social relationship pathways).
- What makes language *do anything* are not the words but the total external social contexts that cannot be seen in the moment of conversation.

If you think of discourse analysis in broad terms like this, the slightly different approaches to discourse analysis will make more sense. These approaches occur across all the social sciences, so read them all. My synthesized versions are in Guerin (1997, 2003b, 2004, 2016a), which have the advantage that I present ways of doing social analysis as part of the discourse analysis, and most others do not have much detail about this.

How sensitive is language use to social contexts?

When the colour of a chameleon's background environment changes, perhaps the sun comes out or it moves to a different foliage, then its skin colour can change because of specialized guanine crystals. This has been utilized over time for protection from predators and for chameleon social behaviour. Because of these possible changes in appearance, chameleons can thwart predators and get other chameleons to change their behaviour. Pretty smart, eh?

Now consider what you might do if *you* met a 'predator'? Walking alone in a small dark and deserted alley and someone confronts you and threatens you in some way. What do you do? Or, what *can* you do?

You could run away, or you could physically fight or repel them in some way. But more likely, you would first use a variety of *language strategies*: scream, yell out, negotiate, talk them down, distract them, talk defiantly and brazenly at them, offer them something, make a joke, try and phone the police quickly, or beg for mercy.

The more you study language strategies the more impressed you get at what a hugely flexible and variable set of behaviours we have learned, but you also need to remember that it is the social contexts, behaviours, and consequences that are doing all the hard work of making things actually happen, not the words themselves. In the dark alley you probably have little in the way of social power—no reciprocities or a history of resource reciprocity with the person confronting you—to make your words actually do something. Your words will 'fall on deaf ears'. Remember that words themselves have no power, just your social contexts of resources and reciprocities. If you noticed that the person was a second cousin of yours, that would be different! You now have historical reciprocities in your social relationships to give more 'power' to your words to change the person's behaviour. But the problem with strangers in a dark alley is that they have no reason to do what you say.

The nuances and sensitivities of language are therefore really the sensitivities of our social behaviours and social relationship contexts, but language is a key way we *do* our social behaviours. In fact, it is now probably the most frequent way we behave socially. With the ways in which our social relationships have changed in modernity from mostly family to mostly strangers (see Guerin, 2016a), we have less other ties with the people around us that we might use to enact our social life, and money is the main reciprocity and power of language now—asking people to do things for you often only works now by exchanging money (except with family and friends usually). Money might work with the stranger in the alley above, for example, "Here, take my wallet but please don't hurt me!"

Sociolinguistics, sociologists, and some social psychologists have for a long time been documenting these language strategies and what they can do in different contexts (summarized in Guerin, 1997). Hypnotherapists have long been using and adapting these, as have marketing salespeople. In the case of hypnotherapists, they have some professional 'power' to get people to do things, but the salesperson is starting from little power except 'raw speech' and perhaps the degree to which the customer needs to buy whatever it is on sale. In modernity, they are not likely to know their customers or be related to them, but they still use those language strategies anyway: "Hello my friend, what can I do for you?"; "Hey bro, and what are you after today?"; "I really like you, so let me make a special deal just for you". Chameleons changing colour ...

Details of the social sensitivities can be found in sociolinguistic and other research or work backwards from my summaries of the social science literatures (see Guerin, 1997, 2004, 2016a).

What are the functions of the main parts of language?

The main 'structures' of language use in sociolinguistics are grammar, syntax, morphology, phonology, semantics, and pragmatics. From what will be said later (V5.2), these are called 'structures' because there is some repetition and patterning found, but this repetition can be due to a number of things. Each different language or variation on a language (dialect) has different versions of each of these, although there are still common patterns. But remember, finding a common pattern or 'structure' does not mean it must be genetically programmed into human beings, because we also all share very patterned environments, especially social environments. I have repeatedly emphasized that the words (and now structures) are not as important as what the social behaviours do for us and what the outcomes of those might be. So patterns can occur because of common ways we adapt to the life resources to be gained by talking with people—Pathway 2.

I contend that there are two major functions (and I am not the first to say this of course) that occur in our uses of language, and both are shaped by our social environments along the Pathway 2 fork in the road (Guerin, 1997). First, some of the patterning is due to common ways we get resources through people and communities, and we need to have patterns to make this work properly. This is about semantics and pragmatics. There is no use going to a grocery store and asking to buy a 'watermelon' when you want some bread, nor is it any use asking for a 'scibboard' when you want some bread. If we change the words we have been trained to use, or just make up new ones, then language will no longer function. Listeners will not know what they are supposed to do (regardless of whether they will do it anyway).

If you think about language use, as I do, as a really neat way of getting people to do things (but only if the resource reciprocity contexts are right), then you need a stable and repetitive set of language behaviours. So, we would expect to find 'structures' in our semantics and pragmatics.

So, each language group or linguistic community ends up with a *patterned* set of words, a vocabulary, which they are trained over many years to use in context. These patterns change, like all structures, but in this case fairly slowly. There are subgroups who use words others do not know, and old words that are no longer used. Meanings (semantics, or 'what we have been trained to do when we hear words') also change, for example "flirt" once referred to a sudden movement, usually to hit someone or sneer at them.

The second type of repetition or structure in language use refers to syntax, morphology, and phonology. These can be thought of as patterns that do not get people to do particular things, but patterns that make any language use *faster* and *more accurate*. If you leave all the grammar out of what you say, people will understand you (like Mandarin characters) but it will be slow and inaccurate. If you change the phonology people might also understand, but it will be slow and inaccurate (guesswork). For most English speakers, you just need to listen to a thick Scottish or a southern US phonology to get the point. And vice versa for people living in Scotland or the southern United States. They can keep the syntax and morphology the same as 'your' English, but the changed phonology throws you off; it *slows down* getting people to do things you say and leads to *more mistakes*. You keep asking them to repeat again what they said (in English) but slower.

As exercises, listen to some of these same-language different pronunciations online and see how your accuracy and speed are affected. Or in English, try talking normally but use a subject–object–verb (SOV) structure to your sentences: "My cousin a chicken burger ate." Notice that you *can* do this, but that your talking slows down, and your listeners slow down (more so when Yoda talks). And then remember that languages like German do this all the time and really fluently, so you and your listeners would eventually learn to adapt and speed up eventually—once a new patterning is done repetitively. It is possible to make any changes to languages you like, but you need to have them form a repetitive structure and be accepted within a linguistic community for this to be useful (Everett, 2005).

What do we do to people with different forms of language use?

What do people do all day with language? In general, I characterize two forms—getting people to do things directly, and managing social relationships. The first might be asking favours of people, giving rules to be followed, and telling people to do things. Remember that these will only work if the social relationship resources, exchanges, and reciprocities are in place—the words themselves do nothing. Because of this, the second general function of using words is there to manage our social relationships, and this might include breaking the relationship off, telling jokes to friends, telling someone how lovely they look, talking about something you saw on television or in the newspaper, or inviting someone to a picnic. This latter group make up some of the weirdest forms of language, but they are vitally important to our social lives (humour, rituals, gossip, entertainment).

A good exercise to do is to trace during a day or two all the forms of language you use in these categories. All the while also trace who is the audience, what is your relationship with the audience, and what you exchange or reciprocate with the audience. You will learn a lot about yourself if you do this thoroughly. Remember that you are not just tracing your language patterns but your patterns of different social relationships.

What are the main types of language we use?

First, there is everything that is currently called 'cognition' within psychology, and all of the events we call 'thinking'. But I will deal with these in the next chapter as they commonly seem different (and they indeed have special properties compared to language spoken out loud). For example, everything we call 'memory' or recall is really about language use, and therefore inherently depends on the social context not on whether it is true or false. These forms include thinking, consciousness, discernment, hearing voices, and rumination.

Second, there are uses of language to get people to do things. Common forms in our lives are friends and family asking (or demanding) that people do things, and perhaps just as commonly people at work (colleagues and other stranger relationships) getting you to do things for your job. As we will see later, all these change over time depending upon the social relationships and histories involved.

Third, there are other forms of using language to get people to do things, but ones that work through *written* rules and enforced (words need the social relationship consequences to have any effect remember) through corporations and businesses where you work, law courts, governments, police, civil service, schools, colleges, and universities, etc. These are the bureaucratic forms enforced through government or corporate social consequences (V5.1).

Fourth, there are forms of talk that purport to be directly reporting about the world and its consequences with the (purported) aim of letting listeners follow these (true) rules about the world to do things correctly or save them from bad consequences. These include science statements, medical stories, lectures, and all the myriad of ways we explain things to other people in everyday life and present our beliefs (V5.5).

Fifth, there are the forms that are there mainly (or completely) to manage our social relationships. These can be strange because the content of what is said is not the important thing about such uses of language. But at the same time, they are not frivolous or useless because if we do not manage our social relationships (whether kin, friends, or strangers), then all our resources will fade away and our other talk will have no effects anyway. So, whereas such talk as rituals, jokes, and gossiping might seem frivolous, it is important. But because such talk can be about almost anything, it might sometimes hurt other people, so we need to be careful with it (Guerin, 2003a). Such forms also include all the entertaining talk and on the larger scale we have literature, novels, poetry, oratory, songs, and theatre. We also have ritualized talk, myth telling, other forms of storytelling and narrative, indigenous and spiritual knowledges, rumour, and gossip.

Sixth, is the form of talking about who you are and what your life plans and goals are. There is a lot of 'self-talk' but this is not really a direct report of your 'self' but a mixture of doing things to people to have them do things (our first and second categories above) and also of managing your social relationships because you are telling these stories about yourself. So, it is a mixture but is frequently used to deal with your social relationships (V5.5).

All these forms of talk get mixed up, but whether they work or not, as I keep reminding you, depends on your social relationships and the context—not the words themselves. The situation of a government trying to enforce the words, "Do not drive over 50 kph here", is very different from saying to a friend, "Can you pass me the salt?"

References

I have also included here those authors I have learned from to compile the material in this chapter (whether I agreed with them or not), but not explicitly cited herein.

Ardener, E. (Ed.) (1971). *Social anthropology and language*. London: Tavistock.
Battye, V., & Moss, P. (1978). *Private talk: A study of monologue*. Melbourne: Australian International Press.
Bentley, A. F. (1935). *Behavior knowledge fact*. Bloomington, IN: Principia Press.
Berk, L. E., & Winsler, A. (1995). *Scaffolding children's learning: Vygotsky and early childhood education*. Washington, DC: National Association for the Education of Young Children.
Billig, M. (2008). The language of critical discourse analysis. *Discourse & Society*, *19*, 783–800.

Burman, E., & Parker, I. (1993). *Discourse analytic research: Repertoires and readings of texts in action.* London: Routledge.

Coward, R., & Ellis, J. (1977). *Language and materialism: Developments in semiology ad the theory of the subject.* London: Routledge & Kegan Paul.

Deleuze, G. (1995). *Negotiations 1972–1990.* New York, NY: Columbia University Press.

Edwards, D. (1997). *Discourse and cognition.* London: Sage.

Edwards, D., & Potter, J. (1993). Language and causation: A discursive action model of description and attribution. *Psychological Review, 100,* 23–41.

Eggins, S., & Slade, D. (1997). *Analysing casual conversations.* London: Cassell.

Erickson, F. (2004). *Talk and social theory: Ecologies of speaking and listening in everyday life.* London: Polity Press.

Everett, D. (2005). Cultural constraints on grammar and cognition in Pirahã. *Current Anthropology, 46,* 621–646.

Fraser, B. (1990). Perspectives on politeness. *Journal of Pragmatics, 14,* 219–236.

Guerin, B. (1997). Social contexts for communication: Communicative power as past and present social consequences. In J. Owen (Ed.), *Context and communication behavior* (pp. 133–179). Reno, NV: Context Press.

Guerin, B. (2003a). Combating prejudice and racism: New interventions from a functional analysis of racist language. *Journal of Community and Applied Social Psychology, 13,* 29–45.

Guerin, B. (2003b). Language use as social strategy: A review and an analytic framework for the social sciences. *Review of General Psychology, 7,* 251–298.

Guerin, B. (2004). *Handbook for analyzing the social strategies of everyday life.* Reno, NV: Context Press.

Guerin, B. (2016a). *How to rethink human behavior: A practical guide to social contextual analysis.* London: Routledge.

Guerin, B. (2016b). *How to rethink psychology: New metaphors for understanding people and their behavior.* London: Routledge.

Guerin, B. (2017). *How to rethink mental illness: The human contexts behind the labels.* London: Routledge.

Guerin, B. (2020). What does poetry do to readers and listeners, and how does it do this? Language use as social activity and its clinical relevance. *Revista Brasileira de Análise do Comportamento, 15.*

Harré, R. (1976). *Life sentences: Aspects of the social role of language.* New York, NY: John Wiley.

Hekman, S. (2010). *The material of knowledge: Feminist disclosures.* Bloomington, IN: Indiana University Press.

Jaworski, A., & Coupland, N. (Eds.) (2006). *The discourse reader.* London: Routledge.

Kitzinger, C. (2000). Doing feminist conversation analysis. *Feminism & Psychology, 10,* 163–193.

Loxley, J. (2007). *Performativity.* London: Routledge.

Malinowski, B. (1923). The problem of meaning in primitive languages. In C. K. Ogden & I. A. Richards (Eds.), *The meaning of meaning* (pp. 146–152). London: Routledge & Kegan Paul.

McCarthy-Jones, S., & Fernyhough, C. (2011). The varieties of inner speech: Links between inner speech and psychopathological variables in a sample of young adults. *Consciousness and Cognition, 20,* 1586–1593.

Nash, C. (Ed.) (1990). *Narrative in culture: The uses of storytelling in the sciences, philosophy, and literature.* London: Routledge.

Nietzsche, F. (1967). *The will to power.* London: Penguin.

Ogden, C. K., & Richards, I. A. (1927). *The meaning of meaning: A study of the influence of language upon thought and of the science of symbolism.* New York, NY: Harcourt Brace.

Potter, J. (1996). *Representing reality: Discourse, rhetoric and social construction.* London: Sage.

Rapaport, D. (1955). *Organization and pathology of thought.* New York, NY: Columbia University Press.

Robbins, J., & Rumsey, A. (2008). Introduction: Cultural and linguistic anthropology and the opacity of other minds. *Anthropological Quarterly, 81*(2), 407–420.

Ryle, G. (1949). *The concept of mind.* London: Hutchinson.

Sankoff, G. (1980). *The social life of language.* Philadelphia, PA: University of Pennsylvania Press.

Sartwell, C. (2000). *End of story: Toward and annihilation of language and history.* New York, NY: State University of New York Press.

Shuman, A. (2005). *Other people's stories: Entitlement claims and the critique of empathy.* Chicago, IL: University of Illinois Press.

Silverman, D., & Torode, B. (1980). *The material word: Some theories of language and its limits.* London: Routledge & Kegan Paul.

Tracy, K., & Coupland, N. (Eds). (1991). *Multiple goals in discourse.* Philadelphia, PA: Multilingual Matters.

Vološinov, V. N. (1973). *Marxism and the philosophy of language.* Cambridge, MA: Harvard University Press.

Vygotsky, L. (1997). The historical meaning of the crisis in psychology. In R. W. Rieber & J. Wollock (Eds.), *The collected works of L. S. Vygotsky: Problems of the theory and history of psychology* (pp. 233–343). New York, NY: Plenum Press.

Wagner, R. (1986). *Symbols that stand for themselves.* Chicago, IL: University of Chicago Press.

4   How can thinking possibly originate in our environments?

Thinking is a difficult topic because we are brought up to believe that it clearly and obviously happens *within us*, and, in a never-explained sense, it *is* us—we *are* our thinking. Our legal, political, and religious systems are built on these same assumptions, as is our everyday conversation, e.g. "I was thinking to myself just the other day ..." However, this is a poor description of what is really happening and is only a socially acceptable way of talking (just like "I saw a triangle").

This makes it very difficult for me to argue convincingly that thinking arises out there in our worlds (Pathway 2) and that all the above is wrong. And even if people were to become convinced by my *rational* arguments, it is difficult for them to really observe this, or get a gut feel for it, because the opposite is drummed into us from birth. I shall make an attempt, however. Several actually, including some exercises for you to try as they are a useful way to demonstrate my argument.

The arguments and practical examples that follow are pieced together from various strands written by different authors across the social sciences and philosophies, although I am sure that my very blatant version has not been made in this way before. It is a jigsaw puzzle constructed out of bits, each of which has problems by itself, but that together form this bigger picture. The pieces come from many people and groups: the sociologists Mead and Cooley and those following them, various postmodernist writers, Marxist psychologists such as Vygotsky, from Nietzsche, Geertz, Hodgkiss, Ryle, Deleuze, Skinner, Watson, Bentley and other psychologists, and the early writings of Freud.

Some of the properties of thinking that can help begin to guide you through the rest are as follows:

- Thoughts are not *in* you, they arise as talking through engaging in our many external social contexts or interactions. In the same way as we have seen for language in the last chapter, thoughts arise from discourses in life situations that are sometimes a context for our active conversations and other discourses, but that often never get said out loud (but they are not in our heads).

- All thoughts are intrusive thoughts; we do not 'decide' to have a thought, they happen to us (from the external social worlds of conversation and discourses).

- Thoughts do not control our actions; concurrent talking about what you are doing is common or ubiquitous, but it does not make those things you do happen in the first place (I will come back to this later, as it is difficult to grasp the first or even the second time; also V5.5).

- There are multiple discourses/thoughts constantly being contextualized by our environments, not a single strand as we commonly assume (we might only be 'conscious' of one but we have many going on at the same time, as Freud pointed out). If we have spent time learning the piano then the presence of a piano contextualizes playing a large number of pieces of music although we often cannot sit down and play these.

- We therefore need to *analyse thinking* in the same way as any use of language, through the many contexts of our environments, especially the social environment. We need to analyse thinking with discourse analysis (SALADA, see Chapter 3) even though most of the afforded discourses are not said out loud.

- Thinking is all about talking and so all the properties of talking apply to thinking; but when you do not say things out loud, some social properties become different, and this is why thinking 'feels' different to talking even though it is not. I will discuss later some of the contexts in which we might not say something out loud (see Box 4.1) and how this affects the discourse so that talking seems different to thinking (see Box 4.2).

- Even though thinking is commonly talked about as the quintessential *non-social, private event*, the most in-the-head or in-the-mind thing we can ever do (Pathway 1, Descartes), thinking is really all about engaging with external social relationships and people. Just as we saw in Chapter 3 for talking, the main purpose or use of thinking is doing our social behaviours.

- The ways we commonly talk about and explain our thoughts in everyday life are also language-use social strategies and are not accurate descriptions of what takes place; in the same way that our everyday explanation for how we ride a bike is not an accurate description of what is actually going on.

So, what is thinking?

What we call 'thinking' is the same as what we call 'talking' but with a few differences, which I will get to soon. Talking is shaped and maintained by the people and discourses around us, and the social exchange contexts we are in. In the right contexts (see Chapter 3), talking does things to people. We do a lot of talking and usually have multiple possible things we can say at any time as it is overlearned. Talking is perhaps the most frequent response we make in life and we can say something in almost any situation if required (but see Chapter 7 for the perils of language). We can talk more than we can do any other actions.

The main things we do for our resource–social relationship pathways we do through getting people to do things and cooperating with people. 'We' are defined by what we do in this world and talking is the main part of what we do. Not quite, "I am what I say", because we do some other actions as well. And certainly *not* "I am what I decide to say" since it all just appears from outside us—talking and thinking. Talking therefore becomes like a 'me' because of this.

But there are many contexts in life that afford us these multiple bits of talking, conversations, and other discourses *but in which we do not or cannot say them out loud*. Box 4.1 lists some of the common contexts for this. Apart from these contexts and their concomitant effects (see Box 4.2), there are no differences to talking that is spoken out loud. All the bits of talking are shaped by what we do and to whom and with what effects; they do not originate or arise from 'within' us. And if we do not say them out loud, that in itself is also shaped by the external contexts that are in place, not because a 'me' hidden 'inside' decides not to say them and to keep things secret. And even when we say them out loud, there are other responses we could have said that are not said out loud either. We always can say multiple things because our talk has been shaped by multiple audiences through our lives, especially in modern times with multiple stranger relationships controlling our lives.

What we call thinking, therefore, are all these not-said-out-loud bits of talking, conversation, and other discourses. They have slightly different properties to the talk that is said out loud, but remember that these differences come from the external contexts shaping that they are not said out loud, not from anything else. *Our thoughts can, therefore, also be analysed with discourse analysis in the same way as talk done out loud.* Thoughts are not 'talking to ourselves' since they arise only from the contexts in Box 4.1 (plus there is no independent 'ourselves' apart from our talking, V5.5). They also cannot affect other people unless they *are* said out loud, but they are still responses being shaped by people (Pathway 2). They do indirectly affect people by our *not* saying things out loud, which might have affected them otherwise (sometimes it is better not to blurt everything out loud).

Box 4.1 Contexts in which *not saying out loud* the verbal responses we have been shaped to say in any situation can arise

- If there are simply too many learned verbal responses for the context you are in to 'say' them all (You: "What do you think about the prime minister?" Me: "How long have you got?"). Simply put, you can only say one thing at a time, even if you have a lot of possible responses in that context.

- If there is not enough time (if there is a busy conversation and you cannot 'get a word in edgewise'). This is one reason thoughts *appear* to occur more when you are alone, *even though they occur whether or not you get to blurt them out loud*. You can just observe them better if alone.

- If a verbal response has been learned in a very specific context (your friends are talking about fast cars but the one relevant story you know only makes sense to your family), so you do not say it out loud because it might be punished. But you still 'think' of it (it has been shaped) and could report this afterwards if asked whether you were thinking of that story during the conversation.

- If there is no audience present for the verbal responses (if you are alone perhaps). In such situations it can be suggested that the verbal responses *that normally occur across a large range of your audiences* will be the ones reported if you are suddenly asked, "What are you thinking about?" You can also, of course, talk out loud without an audience present if this has not been punished, as sometimes occurs.

- If the verbal response has been punished in the immediate social context before (but might be said out loud in another social context). "I bit my tongue", in common English slang.

- If the verbal response has been punished in most contexts (repressed?) so that you might need special forms of questioning to remember afterwards that you were even thinking it (was afforded in that context).

- If speaking out loud will be punished (so it remains only as thoughts) because different audiences in your life have shaped *contradictory* verbal responses that you can only safely say out loud in one group or the other but not at the same time.

To give an example, one context for not saying some talking responses out loud is that you have been punished for saying things like that previously in some way (e.g. swearing in front of your family). These language responses *still occur* but previous experience means that in this context they are not said out loud (but you might say them out loud elsewhere to a different audience).

So, this means that if you do discourse analysis (SALADA) on thinking, you might expect to find a lot of talking and conversational comments that have been punished in the past. Which is exactly what Freud found when he started inventing methods to get people to talk *all* their thoughts out loud. However, he reported this in an abstract and evasive way: that an 'unconscious' had *repressed* these thoughts and that his techniques made them 'conscious' (and psychoanalysts believed this all happened 'inside us', Pathway 1, until Lacan perhaps).

But this just means that some external world contexts (the 'unconscious' is just our world contexts and discursive communities) have shaped us to be silent in these circumstances. And Freud's difficult task was to find methods to get people to say more of the things they could say about a topic than just those that they would say out loud. In doing this, he was not battling the person's 'inner world' (Pathway 1) but battling the person's (punishing) external social world that had shaped the talking to not be said out loud (Pathway 2). But there are more reasons for not saying all of our talking out loud than the prior punishing contexts Freud assumed (see Box 4.1).

Some exercises

Thinking is a topic that is usually easier to demonstrate than to talk through. Please try the exercises that follow (although some might be a challenge to organize). I will summarize at the end.

Exercise on overlearning language responses

This is an exercise I have found useful to get a feel for the idea that we always have multiple things we can say about almost anything. For this, you first need to get two willing participants and two identical objects, e.g. two trumpets, two teddy bears, two watermelons, etc. You can adapt this to do by yourself by doing each part consecutively, but it works much better if you are watching two people doing this at the same time.

Simply tell the two participants that you will give them each an object (the same type) and that one of them must *do* as many things as they can with the object (and not talk), and the other must talk about the object as much as possible, say anything they like, or make stories. Then give one object to each person (identical objects remember).

If they are creative, you will normally observe that the second person can keep talking on and on about the object. Within a short time, however, the *doing* person will run out of things to do. This illustrates the point that we are a language-based society and that in any context (almost), we have multiple things we can say, even if we do not get a chance, for one of the reasons given in Box 4.1. We are never usually short of something we can say about anything.

Basic exercise on thinking

Having already stated some of the properties of thinking, keep them in mind as we go through a new way of looking at thinking and some exercises to try.

Imagine the following, and try and make it feel real: imagine carefully, that you are talking to a friend with another friend also present, in a fairly public place. Just as we saw for talking in Chapter 3 and in the previous exercise on overlearning language responses, we have millions of possible things we could say. We have overlearned responding with talk, and in any situation, we have lots we can say. Anything that friend might say, we could answer in several different ways, as described in the last chapter. If there is a problem with the conversation, we can also talk about the weather or make jokes about other mutual friends. So far, everything is normal.

Then this friend suddenly says something disparaging about you; that they found out you made fun of them to someone they know in another context. They say that you are a very bad person who makes fun of them behind their back. Whoa!

Now let us consider three different scenarios, and really try hard to imagine *yourself* in these positions:

1. *Your 'friend' (maybe soon to be ex-friend) stays in front of you. What do you do next?* You have so many things you could ask, say, question, explain, excuse, etc., to the upset friend. Probably, you find yourself saying one or two of these to them, and then continue after that with your new reactions based on how they respond to what you first replied.
2. *Your 'friend' immediately storms off before you can talk but the other friend is still there. What do you do next?* You have so many things you could ask, say, question, explain, excuse, etc., to the upset friend who is gone. Probably, you find yourself saying one or two of these to the other person present but with grammar switched to the third person.

Have you been imagining yourself in these scenarios? The next one is key.

3. *Your 'friend' (maybe ex-friend) immediately storms off with the other person before you can talk, and you are alone. What do you do next?* You have so many things you could ask, say, question, explain, excuse, etc., to the upset friend who is gone. So, what happens? What happens to you now? What is your behaviour?

Probably, you find yourself saying one or two of these but not out loud (you are in a public space remember). But in everyday language we would now report it as: "Probably, you find yourself thinking one or two of these things you would like to say to them".

What this book is saying is that the 'thinking' in the third scenario when by yourself is no different to the first two scenarios: you are responding but no one is present and so you do not respond out loud (we are subtly punished for talking out loud to no one). Your thinking (more like furious 'mind yelling' or an 'exploding brain') is made up of the same language material (discourses, conversational snippets, explanations, excuses, questions) as you would say out loud in the first two scenarios but just not said out loud. And this 'thinking' is no more 'in your head' then when you normally chat to anybody.

Your thinking (discourses, conversational snippets, explanations, excuses, questions) is out there in the social world but you do not respond out loud like we normally do, and because no one is reacting to what you say or think, it will not get shaped into new forms and will be subtly different to taking out loud (see Box 4.2). Your progression of thoughts/discourses will also be subtly different but merely because your ex-friend is not responding at all, having now left. In fact, over the next half an hour you will probably get to respond (not out loud) with all your possible responses, unlike when they stayed with you (cases 1 and 2 above). When you get home, you might even rave and rant to your cat as if they were this soon-to-be ex-friend. The cat does not respond either so your behaviour verges back into not saying out loud (into thinking) and grammar is lost, etc. and your 'thinking aloud' to the cat will be a more complete rendition of all the snippets of discourse rather than full sentences (since the cat does not reply).

The point is that there are in fact some subtle differences between the third scenario and the first two that would make your 'thinking' a little different to your 'talking', but these differences are *only* due to no one being there listening, reacting, or responding. Otherwise they are identical. Box 4.2 lists some of the subtle differences we might find.

Box 4.2 Features of thinking afforded in any context with no listeners

- Your thinking will lose a lot of grammatical features.
- Your thinking will be shorter.
- You would probably also not continue your thinking as a real conversation because there is nothing/no one to react—there is no 'turn-taking' to shape what you say next (but you will get to think more of the responses you have).
- Your thinking therefore will appear more as phrases or 'snippets' of conversational discourses rather than as whole sentences, compared to talking it out loud.
- Any physical persuasion effects (staring wildly at them in shocked disbelief) might disappear as well (but sometimes we grimace and smile on our own).
- The thinking also becomes unmonitorable and this can have both good and bad properties, and might change what is said/ thought. You might 'think' worse things than you would ever have said out loud, even though both were occasioned by the same scenario.

The next 'quick exercise' below allows you to experience all these subtle differences. You talk with someone, but they do not respond *at all*. Your talking in this case also usually verges off into more like 'thinking' and has the subtle changes listed in Box 4.2, like losing grammar and volume. Your talking gradually turns into something like thinking but still aloud.

So, the point is that language use is responding in external contexts, usually social ones. Thinking is no different except it is not said out loud and there can be many reasons why it is not said out loud (see Box 4.1). We will explore these next, but in the third scenario discussed above it was simply because your audience stormed off! By not saying it out loud, however, some subtle differences are introduced that sometimes make our thinking *appear* different to talking, but these are nothing of sub-stance (see Box 4.2). Our everyday talk claims that thinking responses are 'said in your head' or 'thought in your head', but these are not accurate descriptions of what is happening—thinking is just the same as if you had said the discourses out loud. And your brain is involved with thinking *no more and no less* than when you speak it out loud or do anything else, like eating watermelons.

So, keep this 'thought experiment' in mind as you do the exercises that follow, as they are designed to give you the experiences of what happened in the previous exercise example, when your ex-friend stormed off.

Quick exercise

Have a normal conversation (tell a story) with a friend but say part of this out loud and part of it not out loud. Maybe the first half of every sentence is out loud and the second not, or every other sentence do not say out loud. The conversation will be weird and stilted, but you will get the feeling of going from the same material being out loud and then not out loud, and how these and their consequences subtly differ. Alternatively, if you have no friends to help (from making fun of them behind their backs!), pretend on your own that you are telling a long story to a friend and say every other sentence out loud. Do the social properties of Box 4.2 appear?

Big set of exercises

What I will do next is to walk your through several behaviours and please actually do them. Do not read, talk, or think about them and assume you have got it! If you just learn the words, then you almost certainly have *not* understood (see Chapter 7). We will move from (1) actions to (2) talking, and then to (3) thinking. Observe your own behaviour and notice the similarities and differences as you progress through the *actions* to *talking* to *thinking*. Remember Box 4.2.

To really get the idea that thinking arises outside of you and is shaped by your social environment, rather than from within you (at least no more than when eating an orange), try the following progressive exercises.

1. Using 'motor behaviours'

(a) Find a non-word activity you are good at: playing a musical instrument, washing the dishes, drawing with a pen, digging in the garden, etc.

First spend five minutes *doing* this. So actually pick up your trumpet, drums, or guitar, and play. Sit down at the piano and play. Draw a picture of something nearby. Wash the dishes now that are actually in your sink. Dig in your garden. Do this. Actually.

For the next parts really notice what is happening and what is *going wrong* or is *different* compared to what you just did. What was there in place in (a) that made it go right the first time? Some bits of the activities might still work well, so which bits of the activity are not working now?

(b) Now do (a) again but with only half the equipment necessary. So, you might hold the trumpet and play the notes but do not breathe into it. Use the scrubbing brush in the sink as if there were dishes but not actually with dishes. Sit down at a table and move your fingers as if you were at the piano. Draw with a pen but not on paper (in the air). Play your guitar but with one hand only (I do not mean hammering).

(c) Now take *all* the equipment away and try and do the activity once again. Do air guitar and air drums. Go through the motions of washing the dishes, holding nothing. Drawing but no paper or pen!

Follow-up questions: how long did you do each of these (a–c)? Did you stop quicker in the latter tasks? Was (a) the longest time? What exactly went wrong in the activities in (b) and (c) that were okay in the original performance? Did you cut it short? What shaped you to continue longer in (a)?

This exercise with actions gives you the idea of 'environmental support'. The world is affording, supporting, and shaping your behaviour, and if you gradually take that support away it begins to change. And then stop. *Finding out what contexts and consequences in our lives shape our behaviours is the whole idea of social contextual analysis.* (Hint: we saw in Chapter 3 that with language use it is only people who can do the 'supporting', whether out loud or thinking behaviours.)

2. Using talking

Now we do basically the same, but with language behaviours. This is best done with you observing two other people talking and doing the exercise. But that is more difficult to arrange, so you and another person can make it work but you have to observe your own behaviour as you do it.

(a) Find a partner (a compliant friend is best) and have a five-minute conversation about just social things. Nothing academic or taxing, just normal conversation. Maybe ask about their life or family and friends, daily events, the last concert they went to, etc. Let them do most of the talking but you add bits and talk in a natural way, where and when you feel it necessary. Tell them you will be doing weird things next but that they should just do what they might do in real life.

In what follows, observe the following closely:

- What is their reaction?
- How long do they continue talking?
- What drops out of their talking, e.g. grammar, humour, details, full sentences?

- Do they end up just saying nouns and verbs with no grammar, adjectives, or adverbs?
- What exactly made things go wrong (don't just answer, "no feedback", be more detailed)?

(b) Next get them to talk to you again just as before but you *do not respond with any words*. You can use slight facial expressions but no words. Observe them and yourself closely for a few minutes and think about the questions given above.

(c) Now have them talk to you again the same but sit silently *with your back to them*. Get them to try and keep talking regardless.

Follow-up questions: how long did they talk for? What bits dropped out gradually (from a–c)? Piece together what changed also using the questions above.

3. Beginnings of thinking

(a) Now have your partner (maybe someone new) listen to *you talk* for five minutes, just normally. As before except that you do most of the talking. They can add a bit if that helps it flow.

(b) Now you should continue that conversation with your partner *but do not say anything out loud*. Just look at them while you have the conversation but *not out loud*. Observe what changes in your talk/thinking (see Box 4.2). What changes for you? For them? Try doing the same but with a different person who has a different social relationship with you (e.g. a parent).

(c) Now do the same as (b) but when no one is there at all. Not out loud (although it is also useful to experience talking out loud when alone) but have a conversation with a particular friend or someone you know, but without them being there. Direct the conversation so it continues but again notice how your language length, structure, and grammar change.

Follow-up questions: how long did you talk/think for in (b) and (c)? What bits of your language dropped out gradually (a–c)? Piece together what changed.

Exercise for 'serious' thinking and for sampling 'random' thoughts/conversations through a Quaker meeting

We now need to mimic a Quaker meeting. Get a large group of people. Over 20 if possible but you will probably end up with less. Not people who will giggle or mess things up. This will only help you learn if treated seriously.

Quaker meetings normally last for about an hour. The real effects (in my limited experience) happen after at least 15 minutes but longer is better. It can be a powerful experience.

Sit in a circle with no talking or sounds, no fidgeting. Turn off mobile phones and put away any items that might distract you. Puts bags and things in a corner somewhere so no one is holding anything. If there are lots of people, keep the circle idea but you might have people in the front and back rows of the circle. You should be able to see most of the people this way. No movements. Just relaxed. No need to be New Age-ish either.

What to do: just observe yourself through at least 30–60 minutes and remember your thoughts (what you are saying but not out loud). Notice how your thoughts and their relevant audiences/life situations *change* over time. Be clear to everyone that no one will be saying any thoughts out loud, even afterwards. You will not have to discuss your thoughts after the meeting.

Follow-up questions: the following are some questions you should think about to learn more about this experience:

- What happened to your thoughts over time? Think about these thoughts as just some continuing conversations with different people in your life (who are not there).
- Were your thoughts like *you speaking*, as in 3(b) above, or were they like someone else speaking to you?
- Were your thoughts like hearing a real person you know talking or a more generalized voice? (Quakers believe some of these voices are God speaking directly to them, but they must learn to *discern* which ones are and which ones are not. Other cultural groups believe they are the world's voice talking to them, the natural world talking to them, a natural world spirit, or ancestors.)
- What were the thoughts about and what real-life social contexts or situations were thought about?
- Where were they coming from in terms of your life situations (they are not really random, as Freud found out)? Which bits of your life? Did these life situations change over the duration of the meeting?
- Were they about good things or difficult things in your life?
- Were they about conflict situations that are in your real life? Or unresolved situations?
- Any funny ones? Or only issues and problems that still need resolving?
- Did you start hearing a voice(s) that seemed independent of you and your normal conversations; seemed to be talking to you from another 'space'?
- And going back to the earlier exercises above, were the sentences fully formed or shorter, and not structured with grammar, etc.?

- Were there any thoughts *you would never repeat* ever to anyone out loud? Or not to particular people in your life (the ones Freud was after)?
- Were they single phrases or sentences?
- Were there any thoughts that were lots of thoughts in a row, like a longer conversation?
- Were any thoughts a person or voice responding to a thought that 'appeared' to you earlier, more like a dialogue? Was there even turn-taking? Did any thoughts come back later? Who would you have these bits of conversation with?
- *And for you to think about later* ... For all these thoughts you had, was it useful or therapeutic just to sample them and hear more explicitly exactly what you are thinking most of the time? Did any of your life issues seem resolved afterwards? Were there points of view about your life situations that seemed to come from outside you and give you a new perspective?

Sounds and images

You can also do sound/musical events or imaging like the talking events and 'hear' favourite songs or musical excerpts. Follow the Quaker meeting procedure or do it alone, but *let sounds happen* (but not out loud, no singing). Do not direct these like earlier where you might have chosen to 'play' a particular song with your air guitar. Just let any sounds or songs appear, rather than voices like talking/thinking. Do not resist the voices/talking if you cannot ignore them but notice how frequent they are.

Finally

In the earlier exercises you did behaviours (motor activities and talking) and then you did them without their *immediate* consequences. This was repeated with language and talking in real conversation. In the thinking bits, you had conversations without anyone else there at all, but without guiding the thinking, or had a particular conversation with a person in front of you but not out loud. In the last exercises, you sampled from all the discourses and conversations you have had, but some (the most important? the most problematic?) occur more often. Rumination. All the talking or music had no immediate consequences, so what appeared?

If you did most of the exercises you should be able to see that thinking is made up of snippets of normal conversations and all the other discourses that are around us, *out in our worlds*, just like seeing something in our world and talking but these are snippets not said out loud. The big question, then, is: *what are the contexts in life when we do not say our language out loud?* Box 4.1 gives you some ideas about these.

"Why does it feel like 'I am my thoughts' and 'my thoughts control my behaviour'?"

It is common to think of both our thoughts and what we say out loud as 'who we really are'. It is also common to believe that our behaviour is controlled by what we think: we think of what we will do, and then we do it (also see V5.5).

To see why these are *not* true, even when it feels that way, we need to go back to some basics of language use. When discussing 'directives' (Guerin, 2016) in Chapter 3, it was pointed out that it seems like words can just magically make people do things. Most of the time we ask someone to do something and they do it ("Can you please turn the kettle on for me?"). We forget that social reciprocities are needed to make language 'work' and do things to people. If it still seems this way, however, the following points should also be considered:

- The people we ask were frequently going to do it anyway.
- We tend to give directives only to people with whom we have an ongoing reciprocal social relationship and know their typical responses (which is where the 'power' of words really comes from).
- We tend not to ask people to do things directly if they are unlikely to comply (related to reciprocities).
- We tend to ask only reasonable requests and not unusual or difficult requests; for the latter to work we need to use other discursive or reciprocity strategies (pay them some money usually).
- We restrict what we try and ask strangers to do.

We can now apply these to our thinking as well, when it seems as if we are 'telling ourselves' what to do next, when it appears that our thoughts are controlling our actions (Pathway 1 inferences). But remember that our thinking is more like a parallel commentary on what we are doing as if reacting to other people but not said out loud—justifications, excuses, humour, etc. in case someone does comment on what we do. So, our behaviour seems to be controlled by our thinking because:

- We were always going to do it anyway because of the contexts we are in—whether we thought or not.
- Our 'thinking about something before doing it' only occurs with special things we do, most frequently those that have additional social relationship requirements that might need to be responded to afterwards.
- Because we hugely underestimate how much we do in life *without* any concurrent thinking (because when we are not concurrently responding socially in words, we are not 'aware' of this).

- We underestimate occasions on which for social engagement we 'promise ourselves' to do something and it does *not* eventuate; when it does eventuate, the social engagement brings it about not our thinking itself (the thought "I will stop eating chocolate tomorrow" is shaped by other people and through our social conversations, the thinking alone will not stop the eating).

- If we are 'thinking' what we are doing there are no social consequences because it is not out loud, so there is less likelihood we are controlling our actions with the thinking.

So, when we find ourselves talking (not out loud) about what we are doing and what we will do, this 'thinking' is a concurrent running commentary for possible social engagement, not a 'cause' for getting ourselves to accomplish tasks. If it helps at all it will be because of social punishment for 'not doing what we said we would do'.

A final set of exercises

The use of word associations from Jung, Freud, and others shows clearly how we have multiple responses to any situation (but they just used single words), but this deals with very limited and restricted circumstances. Usually in their procedures, a single word was given, for example, 'Mother', and the person was asked to respond with whatever words they can think of, then another, then another, and so on. These would then be analysed for patterns and linked to theory. However, this only views a fraction of our language responding, since words are not a normal unit for language use. Most language use is about bits of conversation rather than single words— remember from Chapter 3 that language use is about doing things to people, not finding names for objects.

As another exercise, get your very patient friend once again, and ask them to think of a word that is a noun or a verb. Any will do. Have them say it out loud and then *you* start saying out loud all your free associations for one or two minutes. That is, just say whatever occurs to you but without editing.

Freud and Jung would want you to respond with single words or maybe two words, but I think a better model of conversation and thinking (conversation not out loud) is to allow what I have been calling snippets of conversations, which could even be a sentence or two that follow from the word given. So, for Freud and Jung, if your friend said "Tomato sauce" they would expect *single* words from you (in fact, they shaped this behaviour, people normally give more in my experience when not told to use single words). With Jung shaping you, you might say, "Spaghetti … pasta … dinner … restaurant … noodles".

I think that realistically for everyday talk and thinking you would actually produce conversational snippets or phrases: "I really like it", "We had it as a kid", "It is often too acidic for my taste", "My mum always says that I hated tomato sauce as a kid but I don't remember that at all!", etc. So, try the following:

(a) Have the friend say a word and then you say out loud to them all your responses. They do not have to be single words remember. Observe yourself, and note the grammar used and how it changes over time, how long you went on for, how the themes change, etc. All the questions from the earlier exercises.

(b) Now have the friend say *another* word and do exactly the same, but this time do not say anything out loud. Just proceed the same but not out loud.

Notice what is different between (a) and (b) in the length of speaking and the number of words, the themes and variations, the grammar, etc. Did you also 'think' of things you might *not* have said to your friend when you had been speaking out loud in (a)? Was grammar left out in (b) as we saw for the earlier exercises?

Remember that this is a bit artificial because normally if you did not say these out loud then there must have been something in your context for this to happen, like the suggestions I gave in Box 4.2. Here I have just asked you in (b) to not say them out loud, but your friend is still there. But the differences you do find are between saying out loud or not.

In reality, language responses in any situation relate to your history of real conversations, real-life situations, and with real people. As we will see in what follows, if you have audiences with opposite views or ways of responding, then your conversations might have contradictions—you say one thing to one group of friends and another to your other group of friends.

So our thinking, therefore, is not really like the word association test— we rarely think single words. What we have learned are *conversational snippets* rather than single words, and so our *thoughts* are actually made up of humorous replies, repartee, conversations we have had, unresolved conversations, ruminations of things to say in bad situations (V6), things we would say back to someone but do not, instructions to people, etc. (Guerin, 2016). This is also what Freud and others meant by unconscious thoughts, but he focused mostly on those thoughts that we do not say out loud purely because they would be punished or have been punished. These he called 'repressed' thoughts that would end up in the unconscious where they would fester.

(c) To get a further feel for this, tell your friend you will show them an object and that they should just say the first and most natural bits of *conversation* that pop into their head, not single words only. Then show them the object and listen. Use some interesting objects or ones they are not familiar with. After they have said the first thing, ask them what else they were thinking about saying when they first saw the object. What you will typically find is that there will be multiple other bits of possible conversations occurring to them when they first see the object. They will say one of these out loud to you, but they will 'know' that others were 'available' simultaneously and later be able to tell you some if you ask.

(d) Other tricks you can try are to mention one of their audiences *just before* you show them the object. So just before you reveal the object say, "I wonder if your mother is watching?" While they will probably say something relevant to that audience you can check that the other conversations were there as well, as 'unconscious thoughts'. If you do this, you start to get a feel for the following points:

  • Their thoughts are more like conversational snippets than single words.
  • They have multiple responses every time.
  • They can say one or two easily (the least unpunished ones?).
  • They will *know* there were more 'available' or 'afforded' but that were not said.
  • If you suggest some common ones, they can report that yes, they *did* think some of those at the same time, but did not say them out loud at the time (they will know there were 'unconscious' thoughts also at the same time).

The other way to check out thoughts is to do all the above but on yourself. It is difficult but you can track your own thoughts over time and see if you can find their real external contexts in some part of your life. Most often the external contexts will be people with whom you have a relationship, and this includes strangers. Often, they will relate to real problem situations, or 'unresolved' resource problems in your life. Try tracking the conversational snippets that are your thoughts over time and work hard on these questions: who is this conversational snippet for? What part of your lifeworld? Who do you imagine is hearing this conversational snippet? Who said this conversational snippet to you in the past? Where have you used this conversational snippet and with whom?

Summary of thinking as the product of a natural social ecology (Pathway 2)

Our language use is a way of doing our social behaviours (see Chapter 2), dealing with people and our life situations, but not a way of dealing directly with the world of things (except through people). When you begin to understand 'thinking' as just your *unspoken* conversation and language responses, which happens because we cannot say all of the ones we have learned out loud, then all the weirder stuff that people do begins to fall in place and make sense.

Whatever might be going on in the life of adult humans, we have been shaped to always have many different verbal ways of responding in any situation, unlike more physical responses. Thinking is therefore just all the unspoken conversational responses you have learned and a natural part of your ways of dealing with people through language, but they are the ones not blurted out loud (see Box 4.2).

So your thoughts are just alternative verbal ways with which you *can* deal with people, *might* deal with people, *have* dealt with people (and now ruminating), or *could possibly* deal with people, but because they are not out loud, they will not have any effect on anyone—they will have no actual consequences except avoidance perhaps, because you were prevented from saying something stupid or offensive.

And that is why thinking is just as important to analyse alongside the things you do say out loud, as Freud discovered. *Thoughts tell us a lot about your dealings and strategies within your social relationships and whole life-world*: the complexities and issues of how we get what we need through the people in our lives while maintaining those relationships, and what of this is able or not to be said aloud.

Taking the social ecology of thinking and talking even further

So typically, in life, we can report (1) what we said out loud (without assuming this report is true because that also depends on the social context at the time), and (2) that there were some verbal responses that were *not* said out loud (our main, critical, conscious or command thinking) but that 'occurred to us' nonetheless. With some special forms of questioning (or with the exercises in this chapter) we can also report, (3) the other thoughts that 'occurred to us' simultaneously but that we could not immediately report.

Which of these responses occur depends not upon the thoughts themselves, or some 'internal' decision, but on the whole social ecology of the other thoughts concurrently shaped and the past consequences for saying those thoughts out loud. So which verbal responses are said out loud or not depends on other external social contexts (Pathway 2), including the verbal responses already made in that same situation. Which ones are said does not depend upon what you choose or decide to do—the external social contexts also shape that. You can find yourself not saying one talking response out loud ('biting your tongue'), but then with a shift in the conversation you blurt it out (detectives and hypnotherapists use this as a technique). But this is the external social ecology controlling the response (what the detectives and hypnotherapists shape), not some brain ecology.

Thoughts (possible verbal responses) sometimes do seem like they are being shaped internally or edited while on a 'queue' for being said (Freud's 'dreamwork', dysfunctional cognitions, etc.). This is all shaped externally, however, if you can look at the full social ecology of what is going on at that time and previous consequences for what is said. The 'editing' and 'dreamwork' do not get done 'inside' us, they are done by our external social contexts. For example (Guerin, 2016), most of the 'editing' of what we say or not is shaped by the punishments we have had for saying certain types of things, so they are left out. But this does not get shaped *in our brains* but *out in our world* and previous conversations we have had.

So stretching this a little further, what we call our 'consciousness' at any moment are those verbal responses *most likely to be said at the time in those contexts*, but that are not (for the many reasons given in this chapter). In the words of Ngũgĩ wa Thiong'o (1980, p. 67): "What is a soul? Just a whispering voice."

Here are three examples of social situations varying our thoughts:

- In *conflict situations* we will be thinking ('conscious of') snippets of stories we might say about the conflict (excuses, condemnations, explanations for what we did, things we would yell at the other person if it were safe).
- In very specific *personal social situations*, our conscious thoughts will be those shaped as specific to that social ecology (when you are your with family then most thoughts will be family-relevant material except for dire non-family matters that have become likely in all our contexts—or if you are bored).
- In *general social situations* (strangers often), our conscious thoughts will be more abstract, generally agreeable, easily said without punishment, or social-relationship enhancing (which includes some disagreeable topics).

It is also important that what we report as our 'conscious' thoughts are not single words but whole snippets of conversation about the ways you *can* deal with people, *might* deal with people, *have* dealt with people, or *could possibly* deal with people. The method of free association should not be about saying the first *word* that you think of, but about the first *bits of conversation* you might blurt out given a chance. The literary method of 'stream of consciousness' is perhaps a better metaphor, a narrative form. Once this is done you can then ask about the contexts for these occurring and what scenarios in life they involve.

References

I have also included here those authors I have learned from to compile the material in this chapter (whether I agreed with them or not), but not explicitly cited herein.

Baudouin, C. (1920). *Suggestion and autosuggestion: A psychological and peda-gogical study based upon the investigations made by the new Nancy School.* London: George Allen & Unwin.

Beck, A. T. (1976). *Cognitive therapy and the emotional disorders.* Madison, CT: International Universities Press.

Bentley, A. F. (1941a). The behavioral superfice. *Psychological Review, 48*, 39–59.

Bentley, A. F. (1941b). The human skin: Philosophy's last line of defence. *Philosophy of Science, 8*, 1–19.

Billig, M. (1997). Freud and Dora: Repressing an oppressed identity. *Theory, Culture & Society, 14*, 29–55.

Brazier, D. (1996). *Zen therapy: Transcending the sorrows of the human mind.* New York, NY: John Wiley.

Breuer, J., & Freud, S. (1895/1974). *Studies on hysteria* (Penguin Freud Library Volume 3). London: Penguin Books.

Buehler, K. (1951). On thought connections. In D. Rapaport (Ed.), *Organization and pathology of thought: Selected sources* (pp. 40–57). New York, NY: Columbia University Press.

Cooley, C. H. (1909). *Social organization.* New York, NY: Charles Scribner's Sons.

Erickson, M. H., Rossi, E. L., & Rossi, S. I. (1976). *Hypnotic realities: The induction of clinical hypnosis and forms of indirect suggestion.* New York, NY: Irvington.

Freud, S. (1900/1975). *The interpretation of dreams* (Penguin Freud Library Volume 4). London: Penguin Books.

Freud, S. (1905/1977). *Fragment of an analysis of a case of hysteria ('Dora').* (Penguin Freud Library Volume 8). London: Penguin Books.

Freud, S. (1909/1979). *Notes upon a case of obsessional neurosis (the 'Rat Man')* (Penguin Freud Library Volume 9). London: Penguin Books.

Freud, S. (1925/1984). Negation. In *On metapsychology* (pp. 437–442) (Penguin Freud Library Volume 11). London: Penguin Books.

Freud, S. (1974/1917). *Introductory lectures on psycho-analysis.* London: Penguin Books.

Geertz, C. (1966). *Person, time, and conduct in Bali: An essay in cultural analysis.* Cultural Report Series No. 14. Detroit, MI: Yale University.

Gibson, J. J. (1979). *The ecological approach to visual perception*. Boston MA: Houghton Mifflin.

Giddens, A. (1990). *The consequence of modernism*. Oxford: Polity Press.

Giddens, A. (1991). *Modernity and self-identity: Self and society in late modern age*. Oxford: Polity Press.

Guerin, B. (1992). Behavior analysis and the social construction of knowledge. *American Psychologist, 47*, 1423–1432.

Guerin, B. (1994). Attitudes and beliefs as verbal behavior. *Behavior Analyst, 17*, 155–163.

Guerin, B. (2001). Replacing catharsis and uncertainty reduction theories with descriptions of the historical and social context. *Review of General Psychology, 5*, 44–61.

Guerin, B. (2016). *How to rethink psychology: New metaphors for understanding people and their behavior*. London: Routledge.

Haley, J. (1973). *Uncommon therapy: The psychiatric techniques of Milton H. Erickson, M.D.* New York, NY: Norton.

Hayes, S. C., & Sackett, C. (2005). Acceptance and commitment therapy. In M. Hersen & J. Rosqvist (Eds.), *Encyclopedia of behavior modification and cognitive behavior therapy. Volume 1: Adult clinical applications* (pp. 1–5). Thousand Oaks, CA: Sage.

Hodgkiss, P. (2011). *The making of the modern mind*. London: Athlone Press.

Horney, K. (1935/1999). *The therapeutic process: Essays & lectures*. London: Yale University Press.

Janet, P. (1919/1925). *Psychological healing: A historical and clinical study*. London: George Allen & Unwin.

Jung, C. G. (1973). *The collected works of C. G. Jung. Volume 2: Experimental researches*. Princeton, NJ: Princeton University Press.

Kahneman, D. (2011). *Thinking, fast and slow*. London: Penguin.

Lévi-Strauss, C. (1966). *The savage mind*. London: Weidenfeld & Nicolson.

Mead, G. H. (1934). *Mind, self, and society from the standpoint of a social behaviorist*. Chicago, IL: University of Chicago Press.

Meyer, A. (1948). *The commonsense psychiatry of Dr. Alfred Meyer*. New York, NY: McGraw Hill.

Nietzsche, F. (1886/1996). *Beyond good and evil: Prelude to a philosophy of the future*. New York, NY: Vintage Books.

Passons, W. R. (1975). *Gestalt approaches in counseling*. New York, NY: Holt, Rinehart & Winston.

Perls, F. S. (1947). *Ego, hunger and aggression*. New York, NY: Vintage Books.

Pietikäinen, S., & Dufva, H. (2006). Voices in discourses: Dialogism, critical discourse analysis and ethnic identity. *Journal of Sociolinguistics, 10*, 205–224.

Ryle, G. (1949). *The concept of mind*. London: Hutchinson.

Ryle, G. (1971). The thinking of thoughts: What is 'Le Penseur' doing? In G. Ryle, *Collected papers. Volume 2: Collected essays 1929–1968* (pp. 480–496). London: Hutchinson.

Thiong'o, N. W. (1980). *Devil on the cross*. London: Penguin.

5 Contextualizing perception
Continuous micro responses focus-engaging with the changing effects of fractal-like environments?

For language use and thinking in the last two chapters, the reaction might have been, "How on earth can they arise from and be determined by our environments?" They spring mysteriously from within us, surely?

For a contextual view of *perception* in this chapter, however, the initial reaction is more likely to be, "How on earth can perception *not* arise from and be determined by our environments?" Obviously, if I see a white duck then that is determined by the environment—in particular, the white duck that is squatting in front of me. What determines whether I see a white duck must surely be whether there is a white duck here or not. Sure, whether I *talk* about the duck or not is about my social contexts, but not the 'seeing' itself surely!

But in Chapter 1, I briefly explained how philosophers and psychologists have wanted to dispute this for centuries (Pathway 1). Their basic idea was that all we can possibly know about this white duck comes from the information given in a two-dimensional image on our retina. But we see a white duck in three dimensions, so it has been inferred from this that we must have added something in the brain or our cognitive systems. We must have enriched the two-dimensional image on our retina. And psychologists will show you a visual illusion that can either look like two people's faces or a white duck (or was that a rabbit?), so again, they ask, the environment cannot fully determine what we see, surely?

In the way I have just stated all this, the common view begins to sound plausible, and academics commonly talk about building *representations* of the world in the brain *before* we are able to construct a perception and 'see' anything. But if you read that previous sentence again, it can also sound a bit strange: you mean that I cannot *see* the white duck sitting in front of me *until* I build a representation of one in my brain. Really? This begins to sound a bit like the triangle mistake from Chapter 1.

There are, however, several misleading words in the basic arguments given above, which I will put in italics below so you can follow these up in what I will say in the rest of the chapter. This follows the arguments in Chapter 1 showing where modern psychology went wrong, and the Gestalt triangle example especially.

> The basic idea was that *all* we can possibly *know* about *this white duck* comes from the *information* given in a *two-dimensional image* on our retina. But we *see* a white duck in three dimensions so we *must* have *added something* in the brain or our cognitive systems.

The terms in italics will all be disputed in what follows, and we need to take a new tack with these sorts of questions:

- What even takes place in 'perception'?
- Why is perception talked about as passive reception rather than active doing?
- What are the events actually taking place?
- Is there a discrete event or process that should be called 'perception'?
- What is the 'purpose' or function of perception?
- Must 'perception' involve making mental or brain representations/ models of what we 'see'?
- Do we even use the two-dimensional image/sensation on the retina at all to 'see'?
- How does 'naming' relate to 'perceiving'?
- Do we really need to 'add' anything to what we 'see'?
- Do we even 'see things', and is that a useful description of perception?
- Or does the description 'see a white duck' only exist in our uses of language?

The hub of the problem: first attempt

Views about perception that go opposite to both common language and the long history of psychology were best stated by James Gibson, whom I mentioned briefly in Chapter 1, but B. F. Skinner (1969), William Powers (1973), Tim Ingold (2000), and others have come close and added other perspectives (from which I have learned).

There are good ways to get your head around this. First, go back to Chapter 1 and the reasoning I gave around the Gestalt (broken) triangle. People say that they "see a triangle" but if you get them to draw it, they will correctly draw the broken triangle. I made an argument separating two very different responses: the social talking about or naming of the triangle (when the gaps in the triangle do not matter), and the 'seeing' of the triangle that is quite accurate (or 'direct') when you are asked to draw it (that is, *do something* with it). These two responses are very different in both their contexts and their outcomes.

So, the same point applies here as in Chapter 1: if we use the words 'seeing' or 'perceiving', are we talking about naming or drawing (or some other action)? This earlier argument suggested that we need to concentrate most on *what is being done when we 'see'* and *what are the outcomes or functions of seeing.* Is the outcome of perception to 'see' the cat so we do not trip over it (*doing* something), or to *say* something about the cat ("Hey, there is a cat there!")? More difficult, are there 'outcomes' of perceiving that change the world? Or is not tripping over the cat already the perceiving itself? Or in the other case, is saying something about the cat already the perceiving itself? Our language is biased to assuming there is a passive reception of sensations, some sort of perceptual 'process', and then we 'see', and then we do something based on that outcome.

Gibson's view was that *perceiving is for doing*, or better, *perceiving is the doing*, and for modern humans, *talking is the most common doing* so we confuse the naming with other forms of doing/perceiving. Just because we move towards things but do not bump into them does not mean that we have to 'see things' in the colloquial way of talking (seeing as naming, as used in philosophy), nor does it mean that we must build a picture or representation (as used in psychology). The differences I am pushing here are between the following:

- How do we 'see the cat' in order that we do not trip over it? Is that even an accurate description of what takes place?
- Can we 'see the cat' and not trip over it but not be able to name it?
- How do we not trip over the cat?
- If we do not bump into the cat but move around it, but we cannot name it, does that still mean that we 'saw a cat'? Why not?
- Is 'saw a cat' even a useful description of what events have taken place, or is it a shorthand social comment suitable only for social conversation (like "I see a triangle" in Chapter 1)?
- "I saw a cat" seems a good description when I *say* the word cat, but not when I move around the cat while busily walking across the room to the kitchen ("Did you just see the cat, you almost trod on it?"; "I *must* have because I moved around it!").
- But in another way, 'I saw a cat' is a poor description since I did not really 'see' much of the cat (not its legs) and I could not describe the cat to you afterwards or draw it properly.

Think about these in the following scenario, and I will now begin to weave 'naming' into the story as a separate (purely social) behaviour. You can walk across the room and not trip over the cat without 'seeing' the cat in the way that we normally talk about (being able to name it). In fact, we do this all the time. Sometimes we comment afterwards, "Oh, I *must* have seen the cat because I did not trip over it", but this is social responding involving language use. Most of the time I can walk around my world and not bump into things or trip over things *without* saying or thinking what all those things are. This means that those contexts in which I *do* name those things I avoided or missed are really social contexts involving social relationships (maybe not wanting to look stupid). But they do not help us walk across the room (it might help to re-read the section in the last chapter titled "Why does it feel like 'I am my thoughts' and 'my thoughts control my behaviour'?").

Life would, in fact, be a mess if we had to name everything in our worlds in order not to collide with them. But can you see where I am headed with this? Much of the time we conflate and confuse 'seeing or avoiding things' with 'naming things', but these are very different with very different properties, and are shaped by very different parts of our world—one the physical world and the other the social world. In particular, 'naming things' is a social event whereas not tripping over the cat does not have to be social. This is really the 'Gestalt triangle' problem all over again—the very problem that started cognitive psychology.

But 'perception' is not a separate process or event betwixt 'registering on the retina' and then carrying out actions (walking across the room successfully or saying what is in your path). This is what Gibson meant, I think, by 'direct perception': *the doing is the seeing*, they are one. But we get confused because a lot of this 'doing' is also about naming and other social responses, and this appears different because it is shaped by our social worlds. 'Perception is doing' can mean both not-tripping-doing and also naming-doing.

Or you can think again about a phototrophic plant that moves towards the sun. If you change the plant's position in your room, the plant moves to face the sun. How can they do this *without* forming a representation of the sun or naming the sun? In the same way as a plant, but far more complex, we learn to respond/do *differentially* in the presence of objects (or situations), but that does not mean we must 'see' those objects in the everyday or psychologist's way of thinking about 'being able to name'.

The argument I am building up to is that what humans do is a far more complex version of what the plant is doing: *responding differentially or discriminatorily in different contexts*. Whether or not there is any naming. Perception is just behaving or responding in the ways we have learned for any specific context. Our perception is about a huge number of responses occurring when there are *changes on our retinas* (not from images or sensations). *We respond to changes on our retinas, not to things, sensations, or images*—that mistake arises from how we talk about our perception wrongly or glibly ("I saw a dog"; "I saw a triangle").

This was exactly an early argument based on research by Gibson (Gibson & Gibson, 1955; see also Bentley, 1943). 'Perception' is not about 'enriching' a weak two-dimensional retinal image *before* we can see anything (before we can step around the cat), but about differentiating what changes in our world (like a fractal or Mandelbrot pattern) when our multitude of *perceptual responses* are changed and varied. With all the many and varied perceptual responses (see p. 97) this must be complex but seeing and doing are seriously complex in any case. (And this is no more complex than requiring representations to be built inside the head in order to store and enrich a two-dimensional retinal image.)

This point is important to counter the argument that we only ever get a flat two-dimensional image on the retina to work with in life, so we must 'go beyond the information given' (Bruner, 1957) or have our brain 'enrich' this flat image (Pathway 1 logic). That is a *passive* version of perception, and Gibson, Skinner, and others repudiated that. Instead, we only 'see' when there is responding. We do not just get a two-dimensional image on the retina; we get a *changing* two-dimensional image on the retina when we move our heads, bodies, necks, eyes, lenses, etc. *And a changing two-dimensional image is three-dimensional.* So the whole notion of perception being a *passive* reception of light waves is what leads us astray in our thinking—going right back to the misguided reflex arc that was transformed into the internal assembly line of cognitive processing.

My real point is that all the arguments for why we need to 'go beyond the information given' by the retina (Chapter 1), only seem plausible because they confuse *talking about* or *naming* what we do ("I see a cat", "I saw the cat and so I did not trip over") with what we do with our eyes and head just *avoiding tripping* while walking. Just like the 'triangle' in Chapter 1. The 'seeing' and the 'not tripping over the cat' are the same events, there is no serial progression here and it would be too slow in any case.

Try this: place you hand palm down just above an interesting textured surface, and then close your eyes (actually, read the next few sentences before closing your eyes). There is nothing jumping up from the surface to your hand. If you then just place your hand very passively on the surface *without moving it*, you usually cannot even 'feel' the surface. To 'feel' that surface, your hand must behave in a particular way. It must be lowered and then touch and rub the surface, or even use your fingers and rub the surface between them, or scratch it with your nails, perhaps. That is, *to 'feel' the surface your hand must move—to perceive is to do.* Better still, your behaving *is* your 'feeling the surface'. And your hand does not construct an image or representation of the surface but brings about different consequences from the different behaviours.

Now, *think about your 'seeing' in the same way.* There are light rays all around, what Gibson called the *ambient optic array,* but until our eyes and body behave and move (and there are many perceptual responses you will find out in what follows) there are no consequences. It is as if the behaviours of our eyes are like the previous exercise with your hand; it is like your eyes actually touch, sample, or explore in an active way—active behaving of a special sort—but otherwise just like your hand feeling a surface. So, this is tricky stuff, but try to think about *looking* as you did *touching* with your hand; your eyes do many different active behaviours and these all have different consequences—it is like we continuously refocus and sample. *If your eye were perfectly still or passive you would not see anything in fact.* There would be no *direct perceptual engagement with the environment* and therefore no effects. And all these perceptual micro responses change the environment for our eyes, they change the ambient optic array.

One upshot of this is weird—*that we do not use sensations to carry out perception.* Humans can focus or attend to 'sensations', such as closing your eyes and being put in front of a strong light source. But those 'sensations' are not involved when we see things around us, or better, when we do not trip over the cat or bump into the wall. This means that one of the key foundations of explaining 'perception' for a few thousand years was broken by Gibson—we do not use sensations by somehow having them *go into* our brains and be used to construct three-dimensional representations of the world before we can see and not bump into things or trip over the cat.

Instead, we have many 'perceptual responses' continuously refocusing like telescopes, with which we have learned to respond *differentially* to all the 'visual array' (Gibson, 1979), which is far more than just the two-dimensional image on our retina (think again of the phototropic plant). We can say that we have 'learned to respond differentially' (Gibson & Gibson, 1955), we have 'learned to discriminate' (Skinner, 1969), or 'our responding patterns have become *attuned* to changes in the visual array' (Gibson, 1979). But remember that none of these is about talking or naming, although in real life this becomes an important, very common addition. But what we do when 'perceiving' changes our world (the ambient array) and that changes what we do next.

When we 'see', therefore, nothing is 'taken inside' of us, or processed, or constructed, or sent down brain or nerve channels. These ideas need to be extinguished but it is very difficult. Rather, our eyes (and body) actively behave in many ways (see p. 97) and doing this engages us in the con-sequential effects of our environments (the ambient light array is now different, and our retinas change). Nothing needs to be taken inside of us and processed; it only appears that way *because* we also talk about things, but that involves social affordances or contingencies not the object affordances. 'Cognitive processing' has really been about the social contingencies of talking/thinking and their particular and peculiar properties.

The hub of the problem: second attempt

Almost all the theories of perception or seeing rely on dubious assumptions of 'internal processing' or something similar. This is based on a faulty inference to answer the paradoxes posed by the Gestalt theorists seen in Chapter 1. But if we remove that faulty inference, what does a contextual or radical behavioural position look like? How can we imagine contextualized perception?

In what follows I have tried to synthesize and extrapolate from the contextual views of perception just discussed: Gibson's 'direct perception', Powers (1973), and the behaviour analytic positions. It is only one way to start thinking about how we can be consistent when we think about perception, some points that need to be included. But a lot more needs to be thought through and developed.

Perception and focus, differentiation, attuning, and discrimination

From these contextual views, perception is not a benign reception of light on the retina. Nor is it about 'taking in' something, somehow, from the retina and then enriching or processing whatever that is (Gibson & Gibson 1955). Perception is not a separate 'process' from 'doing', which supposedly is constructed in the brain, but is a direct part of how we behave, engage with, or alter the environment to do other things. If I pick up a cat sitting on the ground, we do not bother to separate out what my fingers did and what my shoulder did when 'picking up' the cat, although we could if we were focusing on a separate problem ("Where is it safe to put your fingers when you pick up a cat?"). But for historical and other reasons, we always and categorically separate (1) the 'perceptual' responses occurring and (2) the arm responses occurring; we have always treated them as two separate events that the brain joins together somehow. This is the mistake; they are really all together.

So, the first two ways of thinking need to be ruled out, even though something similar makes up almost all models in psychology (see Figure 5.1).

In fact, Gibson has been perhaps the only one in all of psychology history to venture that *nothing* has to be 'taken inside' and built up in order for perception to 'work'. Without this 'taking inside' assumption, we also do

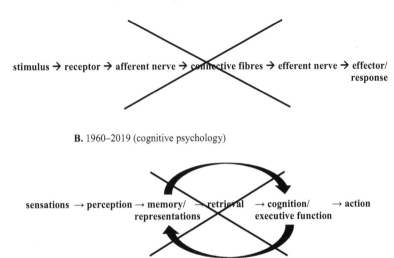

A. 1920s (reflex arc, early behaviourist, early cognitive, functionalists)

stimulus → receptor → afferent nerve → connective fibres → efferent nerve → effector/ response

B. 1960–2019 (cognitive psychology)

sensations → perception → memory/ → retrieval → cognition/ → action
representations   executive function

Figure 5.1 Contextual approaches do not need internal processing chains

not need to assume that we or other animals have to 'store' a representation of the world inside us 'in order to see' (cf. Brooks, 1991, with robots). Out go all the representational models of perception (and most of Western philosophy), which all say that we cannot see without a version of the retinal world enriched and stored inside our heads.

Instead, we need to consider what Gibson called 'direct perception' (cf., Powers, 1973, for a more abstract attempt) and what for behaviour analysis is called discrimination learning or stimulus discrimination. With different things in front of us, and the concurrent changes on the retinas through many active 'perceptual responses', we act or behave differently (and this includes all the perceptual responses and all the bodily responses together). Simply put, that is it! There is no 'inside' process constructing what we see; perception is just our whole body acting directly with the environment; it is all surface and the metaphor of 'depth' is hugely mistaken. Because we sometimes 'see' with very, very little of our bodies moving (especially the case of when the *doing* is *naming things*), the perceptual responses seem like a different process altogether. But in a similar, reversed way, I can also put you in front of a piano with your eyes blindfolded and you can do things. The problem is to explain how we have such nuanced and sensitive actions and behaviours in our different contexts. And the answer is to realize that hundreds of active responses occur to let us 'see' (behave in context). It can hardly be called a passive process!

Types of perceptual responding

So, what are all these active perceptual responses that occur when I do more complex 'seeing' than a phototropic plant? The problem is that the complexity needs to match what has been assumed to be going on inside that enrichment machine—our brains. As Gibson and others were keen to get across, we 'see' with the whole body not just the eyes. And our eyes do not 'see' in the sense of taking in flat retinal images. Instead, *our eyes actively behave in many different ways, which have different consequences, especially when other bodily responses are occurring* (such as moving the legs or talking). Think again of you hand touching something but if it is perfectly still you cannot 'feel'.

We must forget the idea of explaining how we come to 'see objects', since that was a language mistake about what goes on when we name objects without moving other parts of our body. We must instead explain how we move about and do complex things with objects, situations, and people (and this will include social naming sometimes), guided by our eyes' many movements and whole body moving through the world. As Gibson did, we need to explore far more what opportunities the environment *affords* an organism that can move and respond differentially with different outcomes.

Here are some of the ways the body and all its parts move to enable differential outcomes for differential movements:

- eye fixations;
- learned scanning patterns;
- saccadic eye movements;
- changes in ocular musculature;
- retinal visual persistence (<100 ms);
- moving the head;
- focusing the eyes;
- consequential differences between the two eyes (disparity);
- moving the body;
- all the above movements can be three-dimensional;
- colour differentials.

This makes a huge number of combinations of unique movements for all the many and varied objects and situations. The environment affords a huge array of differential responses that change the environment (the ambient optic arrays). So, each person's unique face, each unique part of our world, will afford a unique combination of responses by our body, eyes, musculature, etc., which lead to unique and context-specific outcomes. We can form very complex and detailed responses, but they rely on the movements of our total body (like those listed above), not on complex representations constructed somewhere inside our heads.

The following is not quite true, and a bit simplistic, but it might help you to get the idea. When you look at a specific friend's face, all those movements by all those parts of your eyes and body will be unique. Nothing else (except a clone, and not even a photo) will shape those exact perceptual and other bodily responses you have when looking at this person's face in front of you (we will see next what happens with photographs of your friend's face, which is different). When you look at your mother's face, all those movements by all those parts of the body and eyes will be different and also unique. These distinctive patterns of our own perceptual responding are the 'representations' we have when we 'see'. This is nothing like building a picture somewhere of our friend's face in the brain and matching this picture to the 'information' we are 'taking in'. The actual patterning of active responses *are* the matching, and only occur in one unique environment— when your friend is in front of you.

The next bit of persuasion is a thought experiment and totally unreal (but see Guerin, 1990, 1997). But it might help you understand what I am getting at here, and what I think Gibson was getting at.

Imagine that we could somehow manipulate all those responses just listed: eye fixations, learned scanning patterns, saccadic eye movements, etc. Like the way I can move your hands in the right ways to help you catch a football. Probably impossible to manipulate your saccadic eye movements, and I hope we never get the technology to do that! The point is this: if I could manipulate all your 'perceptual responses' to behave in exactly the same way as they naturally have learned to move and focus when you see your friend's face, then you would report really seeing your friend's face, or act like your friend's face was really in front of you.

It would seem like an amazingly powerful hallucination; as if your friend's face was really there. In fact, the idea is that having these perceptual responses happening is something like what occurs when we 'see a resemblance' between people, mistake someone's face for another person's, hallucinate, dream, etc. 'Seeing a resemblance' of course involves only a few of the same perceptual responses occurring, only part of the unique pattern of responding. The same happens in photos or paintings: the photo or painting shapes many of the perceptual and other responses so they behave in just some of the ways they respond when your friend's face is really in front of you. But there are differences that I will mention later.

Putting this together, the many minute movements of our eyes and bodies, and the vast arrays of invariants that change with all our movements, allows for very complex 'perception' and we do not need to store a picture of this inside us—*the patterns of our multiple respondings are the remembering and these are all shaped by external events.* So, we can walk across the room and not trip over the cat without even 'noticing' or 'naming' the cat. So long as we can have some movements, we can behave in the real three-dimensional world and be afforded new outcomes, hopefully good ones we learn from; we do not need to construct all this from a two-dimensional retinal image and store this somewhere as a representation.

The important point for this book—in fact the very theme of this book—is that this all takes place in the environment and the interface with our moving body, and does not take place in some metaphorical space inside our head. We can again turn psychology inside out (Pathway 2). The complexity of the brain is probably a result of being an interface between the thousands of combinations of *minute movements* (not stimuli or associations) we make that have differential outcomes, affordances, or consequences, but it is not a storage area for representations or pictures of past movements and outcomes. We do not need to build a three-dimensional model inside us somewhere out of a two-dimensional retinal image.

Caveat on methodology

This brings up another important point from Gibson, about how we study perceiving and the methodology for this. Most research considers only simple cases, of people seeing simple stimuli with all the context stripped away (like our Gestalt triangle). Typically, everything else is removed, and, in many cases, the head and body are restrained so that the research participants are focused just on attending to that one simple stimuli.

Gibson pointed out that for his views of perception, such experimental 'preparations' remove all that is important in perception, and we have no idea what is really being studied. But whatever it is, it is not normal perception (what he called 'ecological perception'). The whole point of perception is to move the head, body, eyes, eye musculature, etc., and the more contexts there are in this the better this works. So, by restraining these and removing all the context we are removing the very functioning of perception and are studying something else artificial. And the whole point of perception is to continuously focus and telescope to sample and respond to vast array of changes and details available in the world, so restricting experiments to simple and singular stimuli also removes the very function of perception and ends up studying something else artificial.

The same applies to visual illusions; they do not really prove anything about normal perception (responding differentially in the world as all parts of the body move). Perceptual illusions remove everything we need to 'perceive' in Gibson's sense—texture, depth, detail, etc. The fact that we can see either a vase or two white ducks is irrelevant. If we added any sort of vase texture or white duck texture, we would immediately and 100 per cent see things differently and the 'illusion' would disappear.

The hub of the problem: third attempt

This again means that we must think of perception as a series of actions, events, or micro behaviours we are doing all the time, continuously. We act, for example we move our bodies, and new responses become available or afforded because the ambient optic array on our retinas has changed. But wherever our face and eyes are directed, we can make a lot of other 'movements' to extend this—by moving our bodies or by 'focusing' our perceptual responses.

Another way to start to understand what direct perception is like, is by considering all those small 'perceptual responses' listed earlier in the chapter as *little telescopes that are constantly and independently being focused*—they are engaging with the world or light arrays (like the example of touching with your hand). Gibson (1979) did an excellent job of plotting how ambient light waves changed as a function of how we do all the many perceptual responses just listed. He said that we function with particular responses from particular configurations of all these responses. That is, if our bodies and all the many other actions discussed above keep changing or 'focusing' (like little telescopes), our bigger and more observable responses are 'afforded' by the environment, because we are 'attuned' to them.

The environment or world *affords* us certain configurations of all our responses together, and if we repeat them, we become *attuned* to some of those configurations (we *do things* consistently) (see Figure 5.2).

The light does not 'go into' the head and brain like the reflex arc and cognitive models given earlier; our metaphor of 'depth' is gone, there are only surfaces that change! Perception is only about responses and is directly acting in our worlds, not acting towards models in the head. We do not 'see' stimuli; what we call 'stimuli' are learned specific configurations of those multiple, small, complex sets of perceptual responses and usually only the ones we can name (when responding to our social contexts).

So, perception is about moving and acting with all our bodies, which has consequences for further moving and actions, and the visual array also changes continuously. It is not a passive reception of light. It is always active

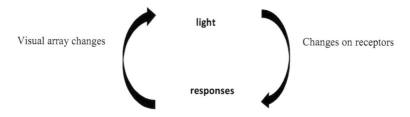

Figure 5.2 Perceptual responses become attuned to changes in the visual array
without processing

and does not need to wait for 'processing' from inside the head to occur (but
that does *appear* to happen when language responding is involved).

There is direct and active engagement with our worlds and with unique
configurations of our multiple concurrent responses, not in a configuration of retinal images or pictorial representations, we find that the more
observable responses occur (and ones that are nameable). But there are
only responses or actions involved in this, not pictures or images that are
matched to previous images.

So weirdly, *there are no stimulus objects or things*, only actions, events,
or responses with the world! No stimuli that are paired with responses
following 'reinforcement', nor discriminative stimuli. There are only ever
active responses that occur or not, and combinations of very complex and
hardly observable responses that 'allow' particular responses to occur in
turn (if the combination is right, as it were).

We do not 'see' stimuli, we behave differentially by engaging with our
worlds. Our 'seeing' is actually a huge number of concurrent responses
that are made, which are barely noticeable but that allow us to do things
(remember to think of all the eye movements as engaging with or even as
'touching' the world of light over time; they are not passively registering
a flat image). The 'end point' of seeing is not a stimulus but responses we
make. No image is produced and kept anywhere in the body, *the environmental affordances or configurations of responses are the remembering*.
Again, we talk about 'seeing things' because of the common function of
verbal responding to, say, nouns.

Perception is like focusing many telescopes at the same time into a fractal world

Another way that might be helpful to understand all this is to think of the
perceptual responses listed earlier as like many small telescopes that can all

'Focusing' and
'telescoping'
(change responding
to differentiate or
discriminate)

Figure 5.3 Focusing is multiple events of changing perceptual and bodily
responses

be varied in and out at the same time and independently (constantly acting).
When certain unique combinations occur, this makes other responses available or afforded (including naming). You directly change your engagement
(responding and consequences) with the world by doing this. You do not
'focus' by taking a single photo and then sending it to the brain for enlarge-
ment and processing—the 'seeing' *is* the doing, and the doing *is* the 'seeing'
(see Figure 5.3).

- Another way to think of this is like a lock with combinations of 'teeth'
  or a numerical combination. But like someone 'picking' the lock,
  we constantly vary or focus our micro responses until a certain combination or configuration allows certain responses we have learned;
  learned combinations open up new affordances.
- Another way is to think of listening to an orchestra. When you first start,
  perhaps as a child or young person, it is like you hear *one* sound; that is,
  you can respond with one response to the one sound (roughly put). As
  you learn more and more, you can 'focus', and hear more things at the
  same time, which can each have new and separate responses. You are
  increasing your differentiation (Gibson & Gibson, 1955) or discriminative responding (behaviour analysis).
- In both cases, we do not 'attend' and 'focus' *in order to* let more
  light in to be processed. What we get or do (responding) from all
  these many 'focusings' *is* the perceiving (hence 'direct perception',
  Gibson, 1979).
- So there are no 'associations' or 'networks' constructed in the brain;
  but rather the differential responding or attunement.
- When we say we 'attend', this means we are doing more of these many
  perceptual responses or at least focus them differently. So in fact all

these perceptual responses are 'focusing' independently and simultaneously, giving a larger range of concurrent responses or events in the body, which *changes* the retinal 'image' and allows all our nuanced responses.

• In these ways, our worlds or environments are like fractals or Mandelbrot sets; we can keep 'tuning' or 'focusing' across all our many perceptual and bodily responses to get new outcomes (see Figure 5.4); once I have learned or become 'attuned' in life, when I walk across a clean room I do not need to do much of this, but I do when walking across a cluttered and messy room with a cat somewhere in there. Remember what listening to an orchestra was like when you first started.

We can also imagine that for babies, they do not 'see' a 'blooming, buzzing confusion' as William James suggested, but they have limited responses initially because they will have just one 'focus'. It would be similar to hearing an orchestra for the very first time; it seems like one sound coming at you and not a 'blooming, buzzing confusion' (unless it is a modern classical piece). You, like the baby, do not come to have a better or clearer picture or sound recording of the music in your head, but rather, gradually learn more and more ways of focusing or responding (including talking). You become *differentiated* in your responding; you do not build a better or more enriched representation in your head (Gibson & Gibson, 1955).

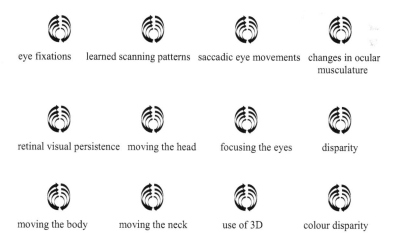

eye fixations   learned scanning patterns   saccadic eye movements   changes in ocular musculature

retinal visual persistence   moving the head   focusing the eyes   disparity

moving the body   moving the neck   use of 3D   colour disparity

Figure 5.4 Perceptual behaving consists of many perceptual and bodily responses

Photos, paintings, hallucinations, and other environmental representations

What about images we seem to see 'in our head', and photographs that we can correctly name ("That photo is of my cat Winky")? Because there are no 'stimuli' or representations of stimuli in your head to 'match' with photos and other images, something different needs to be described when we 'appear' to have 'images in our head' or correctly name photos. Not coincidentally, Gibson also wrote about these, as interesting cases of how we can utilize all our perceptual and bodily response systems as one.

When we try to *image* some object that is not there, perhaps someone's face you know well, we are not recalling or retrieving a representation or a built-up picture of them stored somewhere. What you are doing (how, I do not know) is *redoing* all the responses you previously did when that particular unique configuration of responses really occurred when you were in front of that actual person.

So theoretically, as mentioned above, if you could recreate or re-respond with the identical configuration of the many responses of eyes, lenses, head, etc. listed earlier, then it would seem that you are seeing that person's face even though they are not there (Guerin, 1990, 1997) (and the same for hearing voices; V6.2).

But as Gibson (1971, 1978) wisely pointed out with respect to 'seeing' paintings, photos, and hallucinations, there are still differences so you actually know that it is not the real thing. Foremost of these properties (cf. Boxes 4.1 and 4.2 in Chapter 4) is that you cannot 'explore' the painting, photo, hallucination, or image in the same way as you can when in the presence of the real thing. You cannot just walk behind the object, for example, or focus your eye-lens in another way, and get the same consequences as you do when the real thing is there (although sometimes we accidently try and do this, moving our head in front of a painting to see behind a portrayed object).

A way to get the feel for this is to consider the following:

- If we try 'practising' a piano piece by moving our fingers in the 'correct' way but not at a piano, the piano is not magically there in any sense (we are just re-responding in a *similar* way to when we are at the piano, and nothing more). Some musicians doing this will seem to also 'hear' the notes (remember that hearing is also actively responding and not a passive 'reception' of sound waves).
- Likewise, if we 'think of' or 'image' our mother's face, our mother is not magically there in any sense as a representation (we are just responding in a *similar* way (eye movements, etc.) to when we are really in front of our mother, and nothing more). Some people will

start talking because the perceptual responses are attuned to specific 'mother talking'.

- In both the cases of a mother's face and a piano, our 'imaging' or 'air piano' are subtly different from the full ways or configurations in which we respond when actually at a piano and touching it or when our mother is actually standing in front of us. Many responses are not possible in the same way for 'imaging' or 'air piano' as for the 'real' thing.
- Things get weird when you stand in front of one of those very highly realistic paintings, because while you cannot walk behind it you can focus on more detail (if the painter has done this) and many of our normal *doings* are afforded. I have seen people begin talking to highly realistic sculptures, for example.

If you do not know whether you are 'seeing' a real thing or else an image, a hallucination, a photo, or a painting, try to do things like seeing what is behind it, or focusing on a small section to get more detail. If you do this, your focusing runs out of detail very quickly, and you know it is not real. Whereas, when we are engaging with the real world it is more like a fractal or Mandelbrot set because we can keep finding more and more details, except that we are 'focusing' with many responses simultaneously and not just one. It is far more complex.

The problem for Gibson

Obviously, I admire the work of Gibson, as he battled against assumptions that had not been challenged for centuries. The most difficult part of all this is the problem that I think Gibson missed. Gibson correctly wrote that *perception is doing*, and that we do what the environment affords us, and we do it with all of our bodies not just the eyes. But Gibson and others focused too much on just the functionalities of moving around and not walking into walls. If there is a chair, then the chair affords us 'sitting', as Gibson would say, and we directly perceive these affordances (that is, our many responses *are* the affordance and *are* the perceiving).

But if we go back to Chapter 3, as humans our main consequated behaviours from all these perceptual behaviours are to *name* and *speak*, and this comes about through *social* consequences or affordances of past seeing and naming, not from the objects themselves shaping the language itself. Most of the looking we do in life leads primarily (almost automatically as adults) to naming and talking about what we have 'seen'. This is important obviously, but we mostly now see and then talk about it. Note that we also mostly 'feel' with our hands and then speak, unless perhaps we are 'feeling' whether some clothes are dry.

We commonly believe the ideas of 'sensation' and 'perception' are real because one of the most common behaviours when 'seeing' (attuning to) anything is *naming*, and these nouns gives us the (false) impression that we have constructed something bigger than what our behaviour has consequated ('beyond the information given'). We also get that impression because we do not see the social contexts that lead us to name everything. One glance and we say, "I saw a dog". *But what we name is not the same as what we have 'seen'.* To repeat, seeing is behaving/doing with consequences/ affordances (but with special behaviours).

This is critically important to get a feel for, because this point is the very reason that we end up believing we have concepts and representations processed inside of us and stored as memories somewhere. These cognitive ideas come about (falsely) because looking most frequently leads to talk and naming. *But what we name is not the same as what we have 'seen' if we include all of our 'doings'.* We are confused because our major human affordance for almost anything at all in our worlds, is to talk.

So, the strange position we get to is that we do not 'see' *things* around us. We have constant perceptual and bodily responding that provides differential contexts (affordances) for other responding (such as walking to work), but most commonly we also comment (perhaps not out loud, see Chapter 4) about things (if we have the social contexts to do this). This is why we think that we see 'things' whereas we are really responding differentially.

Non-human animals do the first bit of this very well and can carry out complex sequences without words. We, on the other hand, have the illusion that the chatter that accompanies perceptual responding is actually controlling or directing that perceptual responding. But we could never 'look' quickly enough to run our lives if words were directing our actions.

To get the feel of this you will need a lot of self-observation of how you do things in your world. We do comment all the time on what is going on around us and what we are doing (both talking out loud and thinking), but you need to observe that this commentary is not where behaviour originates—the chatter is not controlling your actions (V5.5). The chatter, as was discussed in Chapters 3 and 4, is about telling other people what is going on, not directing your actions (V5.5). As we will see below, this parallel running commentary is extremely important for our lives as social creatures, but is not necessary to make toast or to walk across the room without stepping on the cat.

References

Bentley, A. F. (1943). The fiction of 'retinal image'. In A. F. Bentley, *Inquiry into inquiries: Essays in social theory* (pp. 268–285). Westport, CT: Greenwood Press.

Brooks, R. A. (1991). Intelligence without representation. *Artificial Intelligence, 47*, 139–159.

Bruner, J. S. (1957). Going beyond the information given. In H. E. Gruber, K. R. Hammond, & R. Jessor (Eds.), *Contemporary approaches to cognition* (pp. 41–69). Cambridge, MA: Harvard University Press.

Gibson, J. J. (1971). On the relation between hallucination and perception. *Leonardo, 3*, 425–427.

Gibson, J. J. (1978). The ecological approach to the visual perception of picture. *Leonardo, 11*, 227–235.

Gibson, J. J. (1979). *An ecological approach to visual perception.* Boston, MA: Houghton Mifflin.

Gibson, J. J., & Gibson, E. J. (1955). Perceptual learning: Differentiation or enrichment? *Psychological Review, 62*, 32–41.

Guerin, B. (1990). Gibson, Skinner, and perceptual responses. *Behavior and Philosophy, 18*, 43–54.

Guerin, B. (1997). Precurrent attentional behaviors as a basis for 'short-term visual remembering': An attempt at methodology. *Experimental Analysis of Human Behavior Bulletin, 15*, 24–27.

Ingold, T. (2000). *The perception of the environment: Essays on livelihood, dwelling and skill.* London: Routledge.

Powers, W. T. (1973). *Behavior: The control of perception.* Chicago, IL: Aldine de Gruyter.

Skinner, B. F. (1969). *Contingencies of reinforcement: A theoretical analysis.* Englewood Cliffs, NJ: Prentice Hall.

6 Contextualizing emotions
When words fail us

Emotions have a strange history within both psychology and the social sciences. In some periods they have been thought of as 'instinctive reactions' that we all have, they are built into our bodies in some way, we hardly control them, they can take us over, and that there are a fixed number of such 'emotions'. At other times, emotions have been thought of as socially constructed and dependent on social groups, cultures, etc.

The goal here is to (re)contextualize 'emotions' in terms of Pathway 2 (see Chapter 1). They arise from our life contexts and are not like a knee-jerk 'pre-wired' reaction to something. The behaviours themselves might be ones we do not have to learn (like crying), but when and where they appear in context varies (e.g. crying both when happy or when sad). They sometimes can also be used strategically to do things to people and so are like language in this way—to some extent. The main end point is to describe *in what contexts are the emotional behaviours observed* and *what is their outcome on other people?*

The different views of emotion

The main models of emotion in psychology are thinking, consciousness, or experience of 'emotion' (see Figure 6.1). If you know psychology you can recognize the common views, the James–Lange view, etc. To jump to the end, I will view what we *call* emotions as things we do, events, or behaviours, not 'states' we are in and experiencing (as before, 'experiencing' usually means language is involved). They are not special behaviours per se, but they do occur in special circumstances.

Most broadly I will argue that emotional behaviours are behaviours we do when we have no other (functional, context-specific, learned) behaviours, but we need to do something. The very same behaviours can occur at other times directly arising from the context, but when we are in *contexts requiring responding* (e.g. an emergency, when we are overawed,

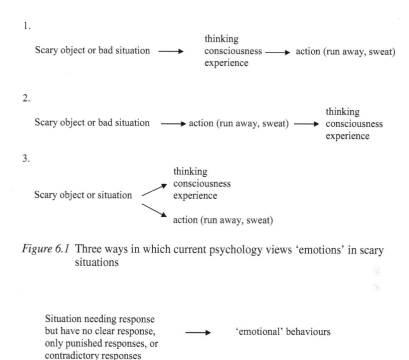

Figure 6.1 Three ways in which current psychology views 'emotions' in scary situations

Figure 6.2 A broad contextualized version of 'emotions'

overcome, something or someone is urging or demanding you act, strong contradictory responses, etc.) but there are no context-specific behaviours we have learned, then we do these. The behaviours themselves are not always of special significance—we can cry when we are really happy, really sad, and in other contexts. There is no need to over-interpret the behaviours themselves (as we will see later for a lot of 'mental health' behaviour; V6). Look to analyse the situations with no clear responses which are producing the emotional behaviours (see Figure 6.2).

So like number 3 in Figure 6.1, the 'experience' of emotion is separate from any 'doing', but the experience is about 'doing' our social relationship contexts by using language or thinking. This is the same as we saw in Chapter 3 for language, that saying "I see a cat" is not about the cat but about the people listening; and we do not learn the word 'cat' from cats. If I see something dangerous (a charging bull), I can run away or not depending upon my history (you might even have been trained to run downhill if chased by a bull). My thinking or 'emotive talk' can occur at the

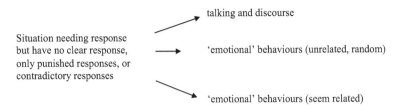

Figure 6.3 The commonly contextualized 'emotional' behaviours

same time, but it is about my discursive communities as it will not help my running. In fact, thinking too much about this situation and what stories we will tell can be more harmful.

So, emotional situations (needing a response but we have none) will now typically produce talking (or thinking if no one is present) and if this is not possible then we get some relevant (to solving) and some irrelevant behaviours (see Figure 6.3).

However, in modern times, there is a problem (V5.1). Most of our responding in life is now with words: commenting, explaining, criticizing, directing, distracting the other person, etc., and we almost *always* can find *something* to say in any situation (see Chapters 3 and 4). A lot of other 'emotional' responses have therefore disappeared because people can usually talk themselves out of bad situations, at least talk so that others do not think them foolish and not in control. If we do not know how to deal with situations, we can talk nonetheless and appear strong in our social relationships, but this does not solve the difficult situation.

As a simple example, I have met people who rarely laugh but appreciate humour nonetheless (I am not talking about people who are just too serious and controlled to find anything funny). When something humorous happens, they use words instead of laughter (but they are sincere): "Oh my, that was funny!" It is when we cannot even have words (or if responding with words is punished) that we emit the laughter sounds. If the humour occurs when on your own (watching a funny movie), then a response is not really demanded so we laugh out loud less. And remember that we also cry as a response to something humorous; the response utilized is almost but not quite arbitrary.

It is not that we have a human 'need' to 'express' our emotional behaviours when we have no other responses, but that the problem situation does not usually get solved if we just talk our way out of it. While crying does not help solve the problem situation directly, it shows us and others that we have no responses to deal with the situation, and that can be important to solving the problem situation (see Figure 6.4).

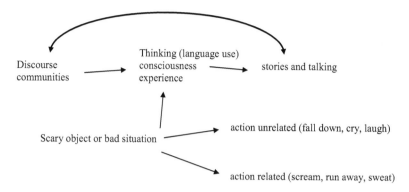

Figure 6.4 Contextualized 'emotions' in scary situations. At the top is 'emotive talk', when we just talk about the situations we are in as our response, but this is really about our social relationships and not dealing with the dilemma situation

There is another important aspect to 'emotional situations'. This is where there *are no words* that will suffice. The key thing is that we need to respond but we have no learned responses, and sometimes we do not even have any words we can use. The following are two examples of this, but there are more:

• When we frequently talk our way out being in such situations, this is only with respect to our social relationships and discursive communities—the situation is still there. This means that we do not learn how to solve a large number of life's dilemmas, since we have spent our lives talking our way out of them, so people do not think we are incapable of solving problems. Sometimes then we are confronted with a bad situation and *no words* will work to distract others.
• In Chapter 7 we will see that language cannot cover, name, or explain everything in life—there are gaps between the world and how we talk about the world. This means that in some situations there are no words for what is happening, and if you have always relied on talking your way out, this time there is nothing you can say.

A first step for getting to this idea is to think of emotions as *verbs* rather than as nouns, to move from thinking about emotions as experienced 'internal states' to being more as fluid *functioning* behaviours. Try saying *emotioning* or *emoting* rather than 'the emotions'. This focuses us on what 'doing emotions' changes in the world. At the least, it provides some behaviour where something is demanded by the situation, even if it does not help.

The second step is to separate out in your analyses these two sorts of events:

- *Emotive discourses*, which *talk* about emotion and this talking changes people's behaviour but through the specialized social effects of talking or writing, not because of the bad or 'un-respondable' situation per se.
- *Emotioning*, which changes the world or changes people's behaviour in a way that affects emotioning in the future.

These two events will have different sources of shaping, different outcomes, and appear in different contexts.

Emotive talk

Emotive discourse is talk 'about' emotions, and functions in several interesting ways as part of language use ("I was feeling really scared"). It has some interesting social properties (cf. Edwards, 1999; Frith & Kitzinger, 1998; Hochschild, 1979; Howard, Tuffin, & Stephens, 2000; Maschio, 1998):

- Like mentalisms, emotive talk is useful because it cannot be monitored (if someone says they feel sad, you cannot just tell them that actually they do *not* feel sad).
- Like all mentalisms, emotive talk is abstract so it can be easily hedged if challenged.
- Emotive talk can sometimes be used as a bluff when using bullying or threats, as your language-use strategy to do something to the listener ("I will cry").
- Emotive talk is shaped by social contexts, since it consists of language uses, so it does not have to necessarily refer to anything concrete at all, and yet it can still work to change a listener's behaviour.

There are specialized outcomes in conversations for emotional talk. The talk is not instinctive but can use 'discourses of instinct' to be more effective ("God help me but I am not going to be able to control myself any longer if you keep doing that!"). A good functional analysis is needed to separate these.

Here are some examples:

- "If you do not put that down immediately I will be very, very angry."
- "I am so happy I met you."
- "This is the happiest day of my life."
- "I just feel like crying most of the time."

Just because they are said and not 'enacted' as emotional behaviour does not necessarily mean they are less intense, less 'authentic', fictitious, or cannot change things in life. They have been shaped to do things to people and they can be effective in doing that whether or not there are emotive behaviours happening at all. I can change your behaviour by saying, "I feel really sad today" whether or not I am actually 'sad'.

Emotional behaviours

Emotional behaviours are also not direct, immediate, or authentic behaviours coming from an instinctive urge or state. These can sometimes also involve language use but not in the same way as emotive discourses (they are shaped differently). For example, you can yell or raise your voice to 'display' anger ("Why don't you LISTEN TO ME FOR ONCE!") but that has been shaped differently to saying calmly, "I am going to get angry if you do not listen to me!" They can be related, but they can also be completely different beasts with opposite or contradictory shaping.

Summary: a contextual approach to emotional behaviours

A functional or contextual view integrates the many 'theories of emotion' from the past theories of psychology. For this approach, what we call emotional behaviours and their outcomes arise from the following:

1. Situations in which we have no already-shaped responses.
2. Situations in which we need to respond in some way (usually to escape bad consequences, but also when overwhelmed by exceptionally good outcomes or in new or overly complex situations).

In particular, we will see that a common situation is an intense event for which a response is required but you have no words, no responding with language (since saying something is our everyday response we can do almost anywhere, anytime).

Such situations might include the following:

- Situations that have very bad outcomes (V6.3).
- Situations that have unexpected outcomes (when your normal response is not appropriate and therefore you have no language available).
- Situations that have multiple but contradictory, powerful outcomes.
- New situations that are highly consequential.
- Social situations, which some people often find difficult to disambiguate.
- Situations in which there has been no prior learning of what can be done.

- Consequential situations in which there are no language responses possible.
- Situations that involve a person with little life experience of learning multiple and flexible responses (like young people).

These situations are not uncommon in everyday life although we usually have some stock language uses ('socially acceptable explanations') we can make that are socially acceptable nonetheless, so not even being able to *say* something at all is less common.

Here are some examples:

- Finding out that you have won an amazingly big and rare prize for something you have done.
- Being told that someone very close to you has passed away suddenly.
- Realizing that you are stuck in a remote place because the person who was supposed to be coming to collect you has completely forgotten about it.
- Walking down the street late at night when you see a gang of young people who are yelling out loud and walking directly towards you.

What are your responses in each case? Which of the ways below would you use? Does it depend upon who is around at the time? Or would your response be the same 'as if' people were around (if these happened to you when alone)?

There are several common ways people normally respond anyway in such unprepared, unlearned, or 'unspeakable' situations. Here are three rough examples:

- We have learned many generic ways of using language to get us out of awkward or bad situations (e.g. talk your way out, give weak but socially acceptable explanations, or bluff); these can be emotional discourses—and these are usually the first things we try in modern life.
- If we have no language uses to respond with in such situations, if they are 'unspeakable', then we can use music, poetry, dance, movement, or art to change the situation (e.g. the blues ... ♩ ♪ ♩ ♫ "Sometimes I feel like a motherless child", or happiness ♩ ♪ ♩ ♫ "Hallelujah! Hallelujah!").
- Failing these, we have a range of generic behaviours that can usually try to change a bad situation even if the outcome is not precise (e.g. crying, yelling or being loud, flailing, talking nonsense, violence, catatonic responses, laughing, running away); these might be random and there is no need to over-interpret and try and find some direct connection (some very bad analyses are produced when this is attempted).

Notice that people cry and scream out loud in *both* overwhelmingly good situations and in bad ones. This is why emotional behaviours are more like 'recycled responses' than specific instinctive emotional reactions tied to particular sections of the brain. In powerful situations with contradictory outcomes but no specifically learned responses, whether these are bad or good situations, we can cry, laugh, flail, etc. We can laugh both when in happy contexts but also in extremely bad contexts (e.g. the laughing of someone 'hysterical').

I contend that we do *not* have a 'flight or fight' response built into our DNA that is 'triggered' in 'emotional situations'. Rather, aggression and running away are responses that *are always available if no other learned behaviours are possible*, and that can often change the situation (though often they make things worse as well). Even in overwhelmingly positive situations, people can move away or flail around in a manner similar to an aggressive response— watch people when they have just received a big lottery win!

So, 'emotional' responses are not instinctive responses but more like 'recycled responses' that commonly lead to *some* sort of change in those bad, 'unspeakable' or unprepared situations. They have not been specifically shaped by that particular situation before, just shaped by bad or 'unspeakable' situations in general, so they look like they are coming from out of the blue (and hence some look 'instinctive' or 'irrational'). The very same behaviour might have a different functioning in another situation but also be used in bad situations where nothing else is possible. Crying is a good example, because we can laugh when happy or sad, but there are others such as flailing, running on the spot, looking away, punching the air, or screaming.

The main point is that an 'emotional' situation is an 'unrespondable' situation but one that needs responding to in order to change it, so we respond with forms of language or any other 'emotional' behaviour or both:

> I once read that hysterical behavior is a reaching out for liberation by means of wild gestures. Unaware of the movements needed to secure their release, animals become hysterical and lose all control. And in their frenzy they often discover the right gesture to gain their freedman.
>
> This reminds me of the liberating advantages of a primitive existence which is purely emotional. However hysterical, the primitive person draws upon so many contradictory feelings that the one capable of bringing about a sense of freedom finally comes to the surface, even if that person does not know it.
>
> (Lispector, 1984, p. 118)

Finally, given my definition of 'mental health behaviours'—those behaviours that arise from bad life situations and for which we cannot easily observe what has shaped them—there will obviously be a lot of emotional behaviours and discourses in what we currently call 'mental health' issues (V3 and V6). Even a quick glance at the *Diagnostic and Statistical Manual of Mental Disorders* (DSM) will demonstrate this, but these behaviours do not arise from a brain disease.

So emotional behaviours are not instinctive or basic behaviours that 'express conflicting inner states', but rather generic behaviours and talk that have been learned elsewhere but can be used in situations in which there are no other behaviours already shaped but the situation demands something happen to change things or escape.

Emotions are often contrasted with thinking, or at least 'rational' forms of thinking (cf. V5.1). This has a long tradition going back to Hume and others, that our behaviour can be controlled by our rationality (thinking, ideas) or our passions (emotion), and passions can often overwhelm our rationality. I am arguing that this is mistaken dichotomy. It is the external context that determines which of these behaviours occur.

Along with others, I consider thinking as *also* arising from our social worlds and strategies (see Chapter 4 and V2); that thinking is language uses that occur in their strategic contexts but are not said out loud. For example in a context where there is something we are trained to say (this can be very subtle, contextually), but we do not say it out loud for many reasons. And of course, if we have no language responses in the situation (nothing rational to do) then other behaviours will occur that will be called emotional behaviours if we need to do something.

Someone can appear rational by responding with language in most bad or unpredictable situations in life, but one day when alone (with no audience) they just start crying. This is not determined by some 'inner' conflict but by the external bad situations. The rational talk was probably managing well to escape any bad situations and protect the person's social relationships in public, and therefore their resource–social relationship pathways. But escape is not the same as solving the problem in the long run: "Everything seems good in my life, but sometimes, especially alone, I just get so sad."

What to do about emotional behaviours?

It has been suggested that emotional behaviours and their outcomes arise from the following:

1. Situations in which we have no already-shaped responses.
2. Situations in which we need to respond in some way (usually to escape bad consequences, but also when overwhelmed by exceptionally good outcomes or good outcomes are continuously blocked over a long time).

Rather than try and describe 'the basic emotions', we can therefore describe the sorts of contexts or life situations in which we might see these emotional behaviours occurring, as listed earlier in the chapter (see also V6.3).

For therapy and other interventions, what should we do about emotional behaviours? If the behaviours are not hurting the person or anyone around them, then maybe you do not have to do anything. Let them cry while knowing that it will not in itself change the situation. However, if the person is being aggressive in their response, something needs to change! As will be suggested for 'mental health' behaviours later in the chapter, we must fix the bad situations rather than try and fix the person. The life dilemmas that I am calling 'emotional situations' are the same, we do not have a response so we produce a lot of self-image talk or sometimes random behaviours like crying and flailing, but in the end we need to go back and work out a solution to the situation itself.

Like all social contextual analyses, we can also tentatively work backwards with 'backwards engineering' (Guerin, 2016), if we are only thinking of possibilities rather than facts. So, for example, if we observe someone with 'emotional behaviours' then we can try and find out the following:

- What is the contradictory, new, or baffling situation for this person?
- What responses do they *not* have that other people might use effectively in the same situation?
- What might they do in this situation other than the emotional behaviours (like the people mentioned earlier in the chapter who always respond to humour with talking and not with laughing or chuckling)?
- What are the hidden contexts they cannot see?
- What social relationships are involved? These can often make it difficult to see what is a correct response if they are convoluted.
- Where does the pressure to respond *at all* arise from? From whom? That might be the real problem. Some therapists pressure their clients respond in some way.

The main ways to be helpful, therefore, might be to do the following:

- Find new responses (although this does not help long term).
- Change the environment (although by the very definition of emotional situations this can be difficult to do).
- Find the source of pressure to respond (reduce some stress by providing contexts in which they do not *have* to respond to whatever the bad situation is).

The last of these often occurs indirectly. The person can deal with living in a bad situation (and you can help work with them on solutions of course) but the real problem is that people (or generalized others) are wanting them to do something about it immediately or to talk about it. They are crying not because of the bad things happening in their life but because other people are requiring them to do something functional and immediately. And sadly, this could be hampering their attempts at bringing about real change in their lives.

For the example of someone crying frequently and indiscriminately, we might try the following:

- When they feel like they are about to cry teach them to sing or play some music, or some other form of distraction (Guerin, 2019).
- Work to discover what in their life are the contexts for crying (recognizing that if it is indiscriminate then it might be larger societal pressures and stresses over which they have little control; V6), and then work to find ways to try and change their engagement with these pressures.
- Crying is likely to be from social contexts requiring some response, so trace who the crying might be for and then reduce the pressure to respond in that social context.

Some examples

Humour

In humorous contexts, we are put in a situation (verbal or slapstick) that has *contradictory* responses, but (socially) some response is needed (the speaker needs you to respond or it could be perceived as being rude). Such contradictions often involve some normally punished behaviour that is presented in a way that the comedian 'gives permission' for you to accept it but all the while your history is one of being punished. This is why a lot of humour necessarily involves taboo topics, and why our sense of humour differs, since taboos differ between people and groups.

So, something rude might be said about a friend that should normally be punished *but the humorous situation allows you to not be punished.* "Of course, we all know Bill, who is so stupid that he just bought a used car off a sheep!" Normally we are punished for making direct fun of Bill but in the humorous context we are allowed to agree or at least not disagree (we are in collusion, in fact). This is also why it is often difficult to know whether to laugh at 'dry' humour, since our collusion with the comedian is not certain. But as soon as the 'dry' comedian gives a smirk or a bit of a smile, we know the collusion is on and laugh.

Our response to this comment being made about Bill in a normal conversation (not presented as humour) would be to take one or another side of the contradiction: "No, don't say that, you are wrong, Bill is smart" or "Yes Bill is a total idiot!" But the first is punished by the comedian and the other people present (our collusion), and the latter will be by Bill if someone tells him (but he has no idea who laughed so you can deny laughing). So, we are therefore *without a clear response*, so other behaviours fill the void—laughter usually—and this absolves you of the collusion with the comedian. People also sometimes react to humour by pulling or turning away, giggling, or looking around to see what others are doing. Some groups use language responses to the comedian such as, "No! Go on, get away with you! Haaha haa", which simultaneously agrees with the comedian while superficially disagreeing to avoid punishment for being rude.

Another language response would be to just respond with, "That wasn't funny, that was stupid", or "Oh, that was very humorous". But this can be punished by the humorous situation in which we are supposed to go along with the proceedings, "Wow, you have no sense of humour do you, how boring are you!" You can also risk having the joke turned against you, "Well then! If you don't think that is funny then please come out the back. My sheep has a truck for sale and wants to discuss it with you!" This runs the risk of damaging the social relationship with the comedian.

But mostly, if the comedian has set the context correctly for us to (1) go along with things (2) that we should not really go along with, then (3) we will laugh, or even cry with humour. We can show annoyance, or some people might turn away or look down as they laugh. And notice that all these emotional responses *change the contradictory situation you are in* (by escape, mainly). We are no longer in a situation of contradictory responses.

Wonderment

In the case of 'wonderment' we are put in a usually good situation (verbal or not) in which we simply have no responses in our previous history, but if someone is present then we are usually expected to respond somehow (remember, in modern life we always are supposed to have something ready to say, however trite). We might be at an outdoor event and suddenly the most amazing fireworks you have ever seen appear it the sky above. What do we do?

If you are all alone then there might not be a pressure to respond at all (try this sometime, be in a 'wonderment' situation while you are all alone and see the difference). You might simply gaze. You also probably have thoughts appear of what you might or will in the future say to others: "Oh wow! I was at the park not expecting anything last Saturday night, when all of a sudden there were these amazing fireworks!"

With others there present with you, there is usually some pressure to respond in some way or another. Most people smile or laugh (the same as for humour but in a different context, so these are actually different functional behaviours). Most of the time, exclamations are made, such as "Wow!" or "OMG!" Many people do other behaviour—laugh, gasp, make surprised faces, sometimes even cry, sing, or wave their hands around. Looking away is common but probably not if there are fireworks. What is being said here is that the actual response itself is almost irrelevant, the important thing is to make some response.

As for any human situation, many people in wonderment situations just talk (but don't you hate it when people do that!). You just start to see the amazing fireworks when they start up: "Oh this is beautiful! It reminds me of that time I was in Hong Kong, did I ever tell you? Well, Sally and I were … "

Those situations we call 'mental health' issues

The situations for behaviour we currently call 'mental health' issues have been defined as bad or contradictory situations in which there are hidden origins in which we do not know why the behaviours are occurring, but we cannot just exit (Guerin, 2017; see also V6). This means that we rarely have words for them or ways to describe what is happening (see Chapter 7). *We do not fit into these bad situations*, they are painful, and we need to change the situation because it is bad, but we have no learned behaviours available. These are the conditions under which the behaviours we call 'mental health behaviours' are seen to arise.

We would therefore expect a lot of the 'emotional behaviours' to occur in these 'mental health' situations because the criteria overlap. But the point to note here is that the 'emotions' are not part of the 'mental health' problems, they actually arise from the bad situation you are in and cannot escape. The situation needs to be changed, not the emotional behaviours observed. The bad life situations lead to both the emotional behaviours *and* the other 'mental health' behaviours (V6.4).

As an example, if you are crying unexpectedly a lot of the time this is because you are in some bad situation in life that needs changing, but you do not have the behaviours to change things, any way of getting help to change it, or even the words to describe it (some people like to call it a 'disorder' because that at least gives them a response to use for what is going on, although nothing really gets changed in your life and the pain will not go away).

When things get very painful or if you are questioned about this by a therapist say (i.e. a response is now required), then 'emotional behaviours' appear because you have no responses to change this situation. Clearly then, the reason you cry *anytime and unexpectedly* in this example, is because your bad situation is *still with you all the time*. If things were only bad for you in a single context you might cry then but not all the time.

Note that if someone in a bad 'mental health' life situation wants to escape by being lethargic, non-responsive to others, disassociated, or avoiding situations, this might be about getting away from the bad situation, but it might also be about getting away from the pressure to respond in some way. Languishing all by yourself does not solve the bad life situation, but it can stop the pressure on you to respond in ways you might not wish to: "If I stay alone I am okay, but as soon as I am with people, anybody, I start crying." The social pressure to respond is as bad as the bad situation itself.

Finally, emotional responses can give us clues that the person's language is no longer 'working' in their social relationships. This could be from not having the language skills, not having the reciprocated social exchanges to make the words work, or both. Having a lot of 'emotional' behaviour can be indicative of many situations, but one is that your words are no longer working, which means the social relationships are no longer working. An exception would be if the bad situation is so general or is societal in nature (V6.7) that no immediate social relationships can possibly help solve it. But even so, words and social relationships can usually help solve or alleviate parts of the problems.

References

Edwards, D. (1999). Emotion discourse. *Culture & Psychology*, 5, 271–291.

Frith, H., & Kitzinger, C. (1998). 'Emotion work' as a participant resource: A feminist analysis of young women's talk-in-interaction. *Sociology*, *32*, 299–320.

Guerin, B. (2016). *How to rethink human behavior: A practical guide to social contextual analysis.* London: Routledge.

Guerin, B. (2017). *How to rethink mental illness: The human contexts behind the labels.* London: Routledge.

Guerin, B. (2019). Contextualizing music to enhance music therapy. *Revista Perspectivas em Análise Comportamento*, *10*, 222–242.

Hochschild, A. R. (1979). Emotion work, feeling rules, and social structure. *American Journal of Sociology*, *85*, 551–575.

Howard, C., Tuffin, K., & Stephens, C. (2000). Unspeakable emotion: A discursive analysis of police talk about reactions to trauma. *Journal of Language and Social Psychology, 19*, 295–314.

Lispector, C. (1984). *Selected chônicas*. New York, NY: New Directions.

Maschio, T. (1998). The narrative and counter-narrative of the gift: Emotional dimensions of ceremonial exchange in southwestern New Britain. *Journal of the Royal Anthropological Institute, 4*, 83–100.

7 The perils of using language in everyday life

The dark side of discourse and thinking

We constantly hear about the benefits of language use for humans, and this is reflected in the huge proportion of our lives that goes into learning to speak at least one language fluently. I want to bring together the other side of the story—*the dark side to language use*, how it messes with our lives and brings new problems. I will also write about the *pleasures* and the useful *powers* of language another time, so remember that some of these pitfalls also have a positive side in some contexts (cf. Sartwell, 2000).

Most of these pitfalls arise from the very nature of language use: (1) that it is a system of behaving that only has any effect on the world between people, (2) that because of this, what is said does not have to relate to anything in the world, because our talk can still have effects and be maintained socially *whatever* we say, and (3) that this social basis is usually hidden from us so it appears that people say 'what they want to' by 'deciding' to do so 'within'.

The 14 pitfalls of language use

1. We confuse words and reality

The first point is that we need to learn to distinguish between responding in the world with words and responding in the world without words. In real life these are very confused and this is truly difficult to sort out. As I have said throughout this book, we are completely overlearned in life to respond first and foremost by saying things. Elsewhere (Guerin, 2017), I have seriously described language as the real matrix (in the sense of the movie), except humans developed it, not aliens, and it has historically been described as having a 'veil of Maya' wrapped over the real world.

The point to learn experientially is that when we encounter things or events we are overlearned to respond in multiple, concurrent ways *with words*. We might also have learned how to respond with the other parts of our body (e.g. touching, lifting, poking), but words come first and usually with several multiple responses (because it turns out we have multiple audiences and spend so much of our time engaged with words).

If, for example, I present you with an out-of-place object, such as you and I being in front of your parents and I suddenly give you a vibrator, you are unlikely to reach for it or touch it but you will have numerous responses with language occurring, and one or two of these might get said out loud.

As we move around our worlds, we continually have language responses, even in the absence of an immediate audience, and we do many fewer other responses. Most do not even get said out loud (see Chapter 4).

It therefore becomes very difficult to distinguish between our responding in the world with words and our responding in the world without words. Our responding with words even begins to substitute for responding without words, and we can act (falsely) as if we have done the actions in the real world but that we can only speak about fluently and regularly. This is why we need 'cognitive' and other therapies, because we are acting as if our language responding is the same as our responding in the world without words, and this can cause problems in our lives, especially our social relationships.

As a demonstration of this, spend a few hours and try learning on the Internet all you can about a skill you have never tried out for real (e.g. rock climbing, throwing pottery, crocheting, golfing). Really study it thoroughly. Then notice how you talk about these activities to other people, especially when they know nothing about them. Does it now seem as if you can or have actually done this activity, even if you have not? It can change your social relationships and people might begin to think of you as an expert. Now imagine the dark side of this, someone with behaviours of paranoia, bad anxiety, or delusions.

> If we ask ourselves what is it that gives the character of strangeness to the substitutive formation and the symptom in schizophrenia, we eventually come to realize that it is the pre-dominance of what has to do with words over what has to do with things.
>
> (Freud, 1915/1984, p. 206)

As a final demonstration, listen to people's conversations and judge how much of what they talk about is describing activities *they have actually done*, and how much is about either activities they have not actually done, talk about what someone else has done, or about other fully language activities such as likes and dislikes, values, attitudes, opinions, gossip, beliefs, etc. And when you get experience in doing this with others, then observe you own conversations. It turns out that we talk a lot about both our talking itself (our beliefs, opinions, explanations, etc.), and a lot about activities we have never actually done.

The upshot is that *our activities in this world are now built primarily on words* and we often treat words *as if they were* the objects and activities they purport to describe. This does not mean that words are bad and doing things is good. Both are functional in different ways. But learning to distinguish between your responding in the world with words and responding in the world without words is one of the most important skills you can teach yourself by careful observations. It will be of importance all through what is to follow. (And try doing this rather than just reading my words and taking about it!)

The following list is to help in this distinguishing task, but basically, if what you are doing is abstract, generalized, passive, can be said clearly or precisely, or needs persuasion, or if repetition produces different consequences each time, then you are likely to be dealing with word events rather than non-word events.

The following points give you a clue that words are being used (behaviour that is shaped by audiences) rather than the real (non-word) reality (behaviour shaped by the consequences of what the world does to you):

- If it is abstract it is probably a word event.
- If it is generalized it is probably a word event.
- If it is active it is probably a non-word event.
- If it is concrete it is probably a non-word event but there are social strategies in which concrete verbal descriptions are used as a ploy to make it seem more real (Potter & Edwards, 1990).
- If it is singular or specific it is probably a non-word event.
- If you repeat the event over and over, are the effects like repeatedly hitting a wall with a brick or does the repetition produce other effects, more like the effects that you get from people when they are bored or exasperated?
- There are good language methods for determining whether someone is lying (a word event) although they are not foolproof (Houston, Flloyd, & Carnicero, 2012).
- If it can be easily or clearly said then it is probably a word event (the real world is messy and complex).
- If it makes a good story then it is probably a word event.
- If it needs a lot of arguments rather than observations then it is likely a word event.
- If you need to be convinced of it then it is likely a word event.

- If the person is looking towards other people during the behaviour then it is probably a word event; if they are looking towards the relevant environment during the behaviour then it might be a non-word event.
- Imagine the person reporting this in front of a judge and jury. Would it hold up in court?

2. False assurances and nonchalance

The first pitfall covers a lot of different situations in life and language. The basic point is that our extensive use of language in everyday life gives us the illusion that once we can name things or talk about things in some way, then we have dealt with them, understood them, covered our bases, feel confident about the situation, or have them under control.

This, however, is totally false and frequently a dangerous illusion, especially in conjunction with a pitfall that I will come to later—*gaps*. Here are some examples for you to ponder:

- "Oh, I know what's happening, this is an earthquake."
- "We have discovered that you have an anxiety disorder."
- "It's ok, it is just your brother and his friends."
- "I looked on the shelf and the coffee is not there."

We typically go around our world full of, and attending to, discourses and phrases that either just name what is around us or give us stories and explanations that we can say later to others. But we will see in what follows that these are highly socially biased and we then never know what we missed. *We end up talking and thinking more in life than observing and sensing*. Our lives float on a sea of conversational snippets and discourses not of our making. And even our observations are then driven by what we can say and thereby make an impact on someone. Language is the real matrix.

3. Restricts our attention (socially)

Following from the above, our attention gets driven heavily by social conversations and discourses rather than by what is in front of our noses (Odell, 2019). We have our attention directed to features arising from our social discourses rather than what is in front of us; from what has been talked about or what we might later talk about. One typical pattern of this pitfall is to view a new scene and only observe until some (socially) interesting feature or object can be named or a story made from it—*then we stop observing altogether*. For example:

- "I saw a dog on the street."
- "There was nothing to see in the park."
- "The fair was not very interesting."
- "We saw that new statue everyone is talking about, wow! I took a photo."

Putting together the first two pitfalls, a lot of our everyday life is 'guided' by our common social discourses and conversations rather than what we might see and engage with right in front of us. Language use becomes substituted for observing and engaging more directly with our world and its consequences. This has several dark effects that will appear in pitfalls that follow.

> Try to forget what objects you have before you—a tree, a house, a field, or whatever. Merely think, "Here is a little square of blue, here an oblong of pink, here a streak of yellow", and paint it just as it looks to you, the exact color and shape, until it gives you your own impression of the scene before you.
>
> (Attributed to Claude Monet)

> To see we must forget the name of the thing we are looking at.
>
> (Attributed to Claude Monet)

4. Language–life gaps

What I mean by gaps is that our words can never actually 'fit' the world perfectly even though we collude otherwise in our communities that it does. If we report, "I saw a dog", this does not actually encapsulate what just happened to us. But this sentence perfectly suffices for everyday talk and explanations, meaning that it can be maintained by social groups and discursive communities as *a description of what happened to us*, even though it is woefully inaccurate as a description of anything that really happened to us. But, as for the *false assurances* pitfall above (2), we can go ahead with our life thinking that we have covered the situation adequately, blissfully unaware of what we missed.

Once again, language use is about consequences from and effects on people, not consequences from dogs or world situations. All the following are functioning to do something to the *listener*, not to do something about the situation in hand or even report some events (see also the lettuce example in V6.6):

- "I had a really fun time at the party last night."
- "He is greedy."
- "I've got this covered, it will be fine."
- "What could possibly go wrong?"
- "I've thought this through and this is what we must do."
- "There are only three ways we can resolve this."

Other examples were given in the first half of this book, because a lot of psychology has taken our everyday (socially acceptable) descriptions of human behaviour and treated them as true descriptions and then worked to find out how they occur—when they were never like that in the first place. Consider the triangle in Chapter 1, a perfect example!

5. Gaps from the world changing

Even if the world could be covered by our words, the world changes continuously. It is difficult to keep changes updated in the social systems of language. The real problem is that if we base the tracking of our world more on remembering words than on observing with our senses, then we are doomed to constantly fall into multiple gaps. This is even true on a small scale when we spend a lot of time looking for a shop we remember from before but that has now closed and some other business is there instead. (Remember that there are good contexts for using words to guide us, but here I wish to point out the pitfalls.)

> Beware! The mind of the believer stagnates. It fails to grow outward into an unlimited, infinite universe … By your belief in granular singularities, you deny all movement. Belief fixes a granular universe and causes that universe to persist. Nothing can be allowed to change because that way your non-moving universe vanishes. But it moves of itself when you do not.
>
> (Herbert, 1984, p. 164)

- "I remember, it is three blocks north of here."
- "I'm sure I remember that it was around here."
- "I don't remember there being any snakes around here, so we will be safe."
- "That wasn't there before."

6. Gaps from observing less with our senses

Coupled with the problems above, the incessant use of and reliance upon language means that our senses get used less since the discursive communities are guiding and shaping our actions with all these words rather than what we might see or otherwise sense right in front of us (unless it makes a good story to tell). We now observe (or take photos) *primarily to have something to say to others*, not to engage with what we might see or hear in the world in front of us. We base our life plans on what we can say and defend to an audience in words.

This is recognized in the many forms or practices that are currently called 'mindfulness'. The real problem is that there are many situations in which we need to rely on our senses more, and some professions or activities train observation skills or general contextual awareness (e.g. the military and context awareness, bird watching). Others aim to reduce our 'verbal chatter' and so increase observation skills (e.g. active sports like tennis). Some examples:

- "The park was boring because I didn't see anything interesting."
- "There was nothing to see that was worth writing home about."
- "I saw nothing, so how come you found all those neat insects and spiders?"
- "It was sitting there the whole time! How come I didn't see it?"

7. Distraction

A related pitfall is being distracted by the ever-present social and community discourses and in this way failing to observe with our senses. This talking-chatter can be useful if you need to be distracted from something around you that is aversive (e.g. being up high for someone scared of heights), but in everyday life it can cause problems (like driving while talking on your phone).

8. Gaps when our normal talk gets challenged

The normal discourses we pick up (and our corresponding 'thinking' therefore) usually are geared to being socially acceptable or having a social impact for us. For example, our common 'explanations' for what happens and how things work are logically and 'scientifically' very weak, but they are sufficient for social discourse, and they exist in our discursive worlds for that very reason. A vivid and partly humorous explanation is better socially than a correct one.

However, there are situations in life when these normally acceptable reasons and explanations get challenged and here the language–life gaps show up clearly. What seems 'dealt with' and closed becomes challenged. This could be someone who verbally challenges what we say when normally our friends all agree with us, someone from a different community or social group who do not let us get away with our usual talk, a researcher or a judge who is trying to look 'dispassionately' at the circumstances (V5.1), or from a competitive situation. Clearly this will be more frequent in the compartmentalized stranger relationships we have in modern Western societies than in kin-based communities.

9. Gaps when we cannot speak or name at all

Another gap that I am finding to be increasingly common, as I explore life situations more, involves situations in which words *cannot* be used but a response is *required* for other reasons (almost exclusively social). A gap appears and we usually fill it in by other means or break down in tears (see Chapter 6).

In most overwhelmingly situations in life, whether negative or positive, in which we have no common ways to describe or explain properly what is happening, we still have a wide range of discursive strategies to 'fill the gap' and usually get away with this socially: the use of mentalisms ("I am overwhelmed"), abstractions, replying with questions, personifications, the use of 'emotive' language, commonly acceptable 'explanations', and distractions. There are also non-discursive responses in everyday life when you cannot respond, such as 'emotional' behaviours other than 'emotive language' (see Chapter 6), crying, escape, violence, poetry, painting, music and other forms of art, and non-language-use forms of distraction.

For example, in a sad crisis situation such as suffering the loss of a loved one, we will commonly do emotional behaviours (crying, hugging) or else socially acceptable emotional discourses: "This is awful", "Words cannot describe what I am going through", "I don't know even what to say" (cf. Guerin, 2019a, 2019b).

The point for this here is that such common situations show how there are more serious language gaps and in these cases, where some response is required nonetheless, non-linguistic behaviours are common. For example, when something really, really good happens but you cannot speak what is happening, you might sing, recite poetry, play music, or dance. For sad events, you might sing the blues or listen to someone else sing them.

The point here is that in extreme sadness or joy words no longer work and the language–life gap is clearly stripped away and revealed.

10. Dissociation

There is a large range of the 'mental health disorders' that involve pitfalls of language based on their social properties (V6.4). If the whole matrix assurances (see pitfall 2) get excessively maintained by discursive communities then the person can start responding almost exclusively on the basis of language discourses and give the 'real' world a total miss.

This dissociation of world and language (where language wins) commonly occurs for short periods during our everyday lives, when we are fully engaged in words (on the phone?) and 'forget' that there is a world around us. But when this interferes with basic living then a 'disorder' is diagnosed. However, the real problem is that language is being shaped by the person's audiences and communities of discourse more strongly than observing the actual world, not any sort of brain problem, and that is also where the solution to disassociation should lie. The language can be strong because the world is totally bad for the person or because contradictory discourses from different people are not allowing a connection to the real world.

With modernity and our focus on words and our multiple audiences that are compartmentalized from each other, it is even easier to begin having (disassociating) discourses that are very specific to one audience but not used at all with the other audiences in our lives. In the social relationships of modernity (late 1800s onwards) we thus have the prototype of 'multiple personalities'. Because language is shaped by people and communities, this pitfall easily occurs in everyday forms.

11. Anxiety, rumination

In a similar way, the combination of our preponderance of doing everything verbally in life where possible and of our multiple compartmentalized social relationships, means that we spend a lot of time with very disparate parts of discourses that will *never* fit all our different audiences and will *never* please everyone (there are gaps). When there is no overarching clear and correct way of 'thinking' these thoughts, we can ruminate them without resolution.

The usual treatment for this is blocking or distracting the anxious thinking rather than showing and resolving the external social discursive origin. The problem is really that action in the world is being prevented because language use has priority over doing and seeing the world, and action is therefore stopped.

12. *Illusions of self*

Our 'self' consists of how we talk about 'our self', what we actually do, and how we report on what we do (V5.5). Some of your 'self' is about what you have accomplished but this usually switches into talking about 'what I have done', which can easily be hedged (see pitfall 1 and rock climbing). As such, the self is mostly about language use and therefore about how we present ourselves and influence all our audiences. With multiple, compartmentalized stranger audiences now predominating in our lives, and a priority for language over what we actually do, language gaps can really screw up any consistent sense of self.

How I present my 'self' and what I can get away with really now depends only upon how good I am at language use. This is seen clearly in social media. Many bad outcomes of this pitfall are strewn around the mental health issues of our times.

13. *Effects of being socially biased*

In all of the previously mentioned pitfalls, our language, and hence our thinking, arises from external discourses and conversations. This means that how we sample these discourses will determine a large part of our thinking, and hence introduces all the biases in our 'beliefs' (see Chapter 8 for more on this). Our social groups and the media often dominate our thoughts.

I recently blogged how after four weeks in Brazil my 'thinking' did not become Portuguese (that would require me to speak the language) but it did change the English of my thinking to Brazilian vowel sounds and intonation. My language and then my thinking was being shaped by my external environment.

14. *Rules (in law, governance, and bureaucracy)*

Our modern lives have become saturated in following words, conversations, and discourses (rather than what is in front of us) to such an extent that we might be excused for wondering if there is still a real world out there beyond words. All the aforementioned pitfalls occur when language becomes entrenched in how we are governed and how we relate to other people and the environment. But I have left the worst until last. Just like Google's plan to map the whole planet into pictures and map locations, I contend that our governments are trying to *map our entire lives and social relationships into written rules and labels*, through bureaucracy, law, and political (V5.1). The goal is to have written descriptions of anything humans can do or say so that these can be put to other uses, such as formulating standard rules of behaviour with punishments attached. This enterprise has all the pitfalls already mentioned (especially the gaps between any words and the world) but governments believe this is the only way we can now run our lives. This has occurred as a reaction to the total invasion of stranger or contract social relationships in our modern world, since there are few kin-based families left to take care of people and track them without written rules.

So, all the problems, chaos, gaps, and pitfalls listed in this chapter are now being enshrined in written-out societal rules and laws that we have to follow or be punished. If you start looking at what goes wrong with our bureaucracies and our legal systems you will find all the examples of *huge gaps* between real life and what is possible, the written language versions of what is supposed to be possible, and what we are forced to try and make possible, even when not in our best interests (Graeber, 2015).

You will not have to look far in law or bureaucracy to see language–life gaps aplenty. Our actual lives and the world can never match the written rules of life according to law and bureaucracy, and (see pitfall 5) they keep changing anyway (cf. Kafka, 1925/2000; Lem, 1973).

> The significance of language for the evolution of culture lies in this, that mankind set up in language a separate world beside the other world, a place it took to be so firmly set that, standing upon it, it could lift the rest of the world off its hinges and make itself master of it. To the extent that man has for long ages believed in the concepts and names of things as *in aeternae veritates* he has appropriated to himself that pride by which he raised himself above the animal: *he really thought that in language he possessed knowledge of the world.*
>
> (Nietzsche, 1878/1996, p. 16, my italics)

> Spiritual arrogance is foreign to our nature and teaching. We never claimed that the power of articulate speech is proof of superiority over "dumb creation"; on the other hand, it is to us a perilous gift. We believe profoundly in silence—the sign of a perfect equilibrium. Silence is the absolute poise or balance of body, mind and spirit.
>
> (Eastman (Ohiyesa), 2003, p. 23)

> In the beginning I had assumed that I was singled out, selected for something unusual. The obstacles in my way? Merely administrative errors; inconvenient, annoying, but no great cause for concern—unavoidable in any bureaucracy.
>
> (Lem, 1973, p. 108)

References

Eastman, C. A. (Ohiyesa) (2003). *The soul of the Indian*. Mineola, NY: Dover.

Freud, S. (1915/1984). *The unconscious* (Penguin Freud Library Volume 11). London: Penguin Books.

Graeber, D. (2015). *The utopia of rules: On technology, stupidity, and the secret joys of bureaucracy*. London: Melville House.

Guerin, B. (2017). *How to rethink mental illness: The human contexts behind the labels*. London: Routledge.

Guerin, B. (2019a). Contextualizing music to enhance music therapy. *Revista Perspectivas em Anályse Comportamento*, *10*, 222–242.

Guerin, B. (2019b). What do therapists and clients talk about when they cannot explain behaviours? How Carl Jung avoided analysing a client's environments by inventing theories. *Revista Perspectivas em Anályse Comportamento*, *10*, 76–97.

Herbert, F. (1984). *Heretics of Dune*. London: New English Library.

Houston, P., Flloyd, M., & Carnicero, S. (2012). *Spy the lie*. New York, NY: Icon.

Kafka, F. (1925/2000). The trial. London: Penguin.

Lem, S. (1973). *Memoirs found in a bathtub*. New York, NY: Harcourt Brace.

Nietzsche, F. (1878/1996). *Human, all too human: A book for free spirits*. London: Cambridge University Press.

Odell, J. (2019). *How to do nothing: Resisting the attention economy*. London: Melville House.

Potter, J., & Edwards, D. (1990). Nigel Lawson's tent: Discourse analysis, attribution theory and the social psychology of fact. *European Journal of Social Psychology*, *20*, 405–424.

Sartwell, C. (2000). *End of story: Toward and annihilation of language and history*. New York, NY: State University of New York Press.

8 Weaning yourself off cognitive models

The cognitive revolution

Cognitive theory in psychology appeared in the 1960s and 1970s (Miller, Galanter, & Pribram, 1960) although the major foundations were built earlier by Herbert Simon in the 1940s. Its use rapidly increased and replaced a series of unwieldy stimulus–response (S–R) behaviourisms (Hull, Spence), loose associationisms, and a variety of other approaches that tried to represent and account for human behaviour, including psychoanalytic approaches that had moved far from Freud and were rigidly enforced through professional associations.

As a psychology student in the late 1970s, for me the cognitive approach was certainly a breath of fresh air. When I specialized in social psychology, it was the main bulwark of any theorizing and this has continued until the present time. Looking back now, having examined almost every theory and idea from psychology and the social sciences, four things strike me.

First, on the positive side, the cognitive theories replaced some very poor theorizing about human behaviour that had gotten out of hand and was not leading anywhere. Applications to real-world issues were difficult and obtuse hypotheses were being generated. The theories at that time were *very* theoretical: S–R links had become tautological, pseudomathematical, with new parameters introduced to fix any problem; associationisms did not have anything concrete to use as a foundation except vague promises of brain processes (Pavlov, Hebb); and psychoanalysis was either wedded to retaining historical ideas at all costs or again adding new hypothetical elements to explain any new findings that did not fit. This is a very broad picture, of course, and there were always some very good researchers and thinkers who were trying to do things a little different within those domains.

The second thing that strikes me, looking back on the 'cognitive revolution', is that there were other foundations that avoided the pitfalls I mentioned in Chapter 1, but that did *not* gain prominence in the way that occurred for cognitive theory (Pathway 2). Two of note are behaviour analysis, started in the 1930s by Skinner (1935), and ecological psychology started in the 1950s by Gibson (1950, 1960, 1966; Gibson & Gibson, 1955). In principle, either of these could have risen to prominence rather than cognitive theory because they replaced the main ideas of S–R behaviourism, associationisms, and psychoanalytic theories in very novel ways, and showed how a new psychology could be built. Ironically, they have each become more prominent in recent times.

The third thing that strikes me now about the 'cognitive revolution', is that the theorizing was actually not that much different to the old S–R behaviourisms or associationisms. They all purported to understand what humans do by suggesting that after humans see things and act, we have some connection, association, link, memory trace, distributed memory, or S–R bond remaining *inside us*. They were all Pathway 1 approaches!

None of these positions grounded these 'bonds' or 'connections' in anything observable, material, or concrete, except promises of brain processes that will be known in the future: we form associations that are in the brain somewhere or just 'stamped in'; we make S–R 'links' through learning that again are in the brain somewhere; or (the new cognitive version) we process information and store this information in some form within the brain somewhere. They all agreed that the world gets 'into' the body through the senses as some form of representation or association and is then stored or left there as some *residue* to assist in future behaviours. That is, despite some applications of cognitive theory to real life, the main new ideas were still not observable and were very abstract—big theories based on meagre observations and not really any different from what they tried to replace.

This leads me to the fourth thing that strikes me now about the 'cognitive revolution': of *why it became so overwhelmingly popular within psychology*, a 'revolution', aside from trying to replace worse theories. For me, there are two parts to this that go together. First, although cognitive theory was not that much different to the earlier theorizing of S–R behaviourisms and associationisms, viewing human behaviour as a *processing* mechanism *inside* people, allowed more structure to be placed upon the woolly ideas about what happened to those associations, links, or connections once they were formed, without having to immediately pin it on proposed brain processes (or give it some other form of physicality). All this was still premised on a future knowledge of brain pathways, but it provided a stronger flexibility for (theoretical) structure to a messy part of the chain.

For cognitive theories, the connections or links are still formed, and they will one day be observable or measurable as brain processes, but before that day arrives, we were finally allowed to talk more about what (might) happen in between by *modelling* or *simulating* these events as an internal, active chain of hypothetical events. There were few limits on this! We see objects and the 'information' about these objects is passed to a (theoretical) processing centre where it can be changed, manipulated, brought into new connections, adjusted, etc. Things can be done to this information inside the human brain independently of the outside world. New processing modules can be added as necessary! It can then be stored so that later effects of that 'information' can be 'explained' in hypothetical metaphors (Guerin, 2016b) of the organism 'retrieving' memories that are also put into the processing unit and a new mix created, completely internally, divorced from the world. It was this (albeit metaphorical) structuring of what happens 'post-association forming' that was sorely lacking in earlier S–R accounts. But the cognitive models, while wonderfully liberating, were all theoretical.

The second part of how I now think about the popularity of cognitive theorizing, stems from the first, and is a direct consequence. All the above is abstract and hypothetical, although still predicated on the future promise of underlying physical brain processes that will match the cognitive processing model. What this also meant was that to build this 'cognitive architecture' was easy. You could add anything on as a new processing unit to deal with aspects of observed behaviour that did not fit; such new units made sense in explaining new findings with the only problem being that they were totally underdetermined with respect to the observable world. They were abstract, hidden inside humans where they did their structural processing, and they had a (promised) future material basis in the brain that meant that you were not constrained in what you could theorize. Doing this was easy, PhDs could do it, you could do it in the bath!

As an example, there is the vast cognitive literature that recognized, quite correctly, that humans seem to deal with the use of language in a different way to how they deal with other behaviours. Instead of wallowing in murky language links, S–R word associations, and 'stamped in' language connections, cognitive theory legitimized the creation of new, hypothetical 'processing units' especially for any observed language behaviour. This went so far as Chomsky's infamous 'linguistic acquisition device', which was purported to be inbuilt for humans at birth and that assisted in the enormously rapid acquisition of language observed in children, *but it was a completely abstract, theoretical, and discursive manoeuvre.*

The point I am making, therefore, is that cognitive theorizing *as a discursive strategy* was cheap to wield, theoretically rapid, and theoretically satisfying (albeit abstract and hypothetical) because it was able to give some credibility to explaining any puzzling aspects of human behaviour that were observed. All said, it was *convenient*, like a 'runabout inference ticket' in logic (Prior, 1960), and the *material guarantor* for this abstractness was the future promise of physical brain structures to come. None of this has changed in 60 years. And each new 'theory', processing mechanism, cognitive structure theory, was seen as progress rather than just replacing one set of words with another without new observations.

So, there were reasons for the cognitive revolution to be popular. This has continued to this day, with psychologists still 'building' totally theoretical internal models of human actions and either being happy as dualists or assuming everything will be explained by material brain processes one day, in the not too distant future. Building the 'architecture' of cognitive processing in abstract models and words also typically followed new developments in computer architecture, which were real.

Weaning yourself off cognitive models by considering new assumptions for alternative ecological, behavioural, or contextual approaches

What follows are six assumptions I have found useful to shake us out of this complacency and backtrack from Pathway 1 to the Gestalt fork in the road, so we can then head off again but along Pathway 2, either as a social contextual approach or something else. Some newer ideas such as 'embodied cognitions' I think are attempting to do this also, but still within the abstract cognitive theorizing of Pathway 1.

These assumptions are not completely in line with either 'standard' behaviour analysis or Gibsonian ecological psychology but can be varied and adapted further of course. For example, I avoid Skinner's use of the term 'reinforcement' as an outcome of behaviour, since it is tautological in observation and adds nothing—if our behaving alters the environment so we are more likely to do something similar again, then let us *describe* that change of the environment rather than just give it the label 'reinforcing' (although this is useful in applied work!). I also have expanded Gibson's ideas elsewhere to include social and language affordances of the environment (see Chapter 5). For adult humans, most of our many environments afford us, first and foremost, talking to others—the telling of stories.

But remember with all this, I am just trying to get some new assumptions out there, and not believing what I propose are the final replacements. But these can help wean you off cognitive theorizing, as they helped me.

Assumption 1

Most 'cognitive' phenomena are really about language use (verbal behaviour). It is very difficult to actually observe the stimulus control of language use with humans, because we just seem to talk without immediate stimuli, we can both talk even when no one is around, and we can 'talk' but not out loud (think). This has led to attributions of minds, psyches, 'mental processes', and 'cognitive processes' throughout the history of psychology. The majority of 'cognitive processes', in this view, are trying to model how humans can use language in adapting to their social worlds. This even includes memory, for example: "Memory, like belief, like all psychological phenomena, is an action; essentially, it is the action of telling a story. Almost always we are concerned here with a linguistic operation, quite independent of our attitude towards the happening" (Janet, 1919/1925, p. 661). So, while the language responses used in cognitive experiments ("Tell us what shape the target was", "I see a triangle") are assumed to be only *substitutes* for the real internal processes of retrieving memories from storage, the behavioural, ecological, and social contextual approaches all suggest that such responses *are* the memories, or better, *are* the remembering. This assumption will become clearer once I begin teasing out the cognitive phenomena into behavioural and contextual terms in more detail in what follows, but if you remember the Gestalt triangle from Chapter 1, the argument is the same. So, most of what are called 'cognitive' phenomena can usually be simply relabelled 'phenomena of language use', and they are real.

Assumption 2

The basis of language use (i.e. cognition) is *social* but this is missed out in cognitive analyses, which has instead employed 'internal' metaphors as their explanations by making some untenable assumptions (see Guerin, 2001a, 2001b, V5.1). Language only works (does things to people) if trained listeners respond in ways they have been taught and shaped to use the language. Language does nothing to the non-human environment or to untrained humans, so we must always consider the social basis of any phenomena involving language use (i.e. 'cognitive processes'). Numerous examples will be given in what follows (see also Chapters 3 and 4). The use of the word 'information', for example, was a theoretical discursive strategy designed to *remove* any connotation of 'social' influences directly on language and thinking (V5.1). This allowed cognitive psychologists to keep it all individualistic, 'inside the head', and with the brain as its (purported) material basis rather than social exchanges (see Chapter 3).

Assumption 3

Analysis of language use requires more detail than contained in Skinner (1957), and Gibson never included our ubiquitous use of language (or any social behaviour) as one of his 'affordances' (even though talking and naming are the most common affordances of perception; we name things and move on). Many behaviour analysts take Skinner's monumental work as a finished product even though it used no research data and gave only rudimentary analyses of the environments that shape language uses. For dealing with the 'cognitive' phenomena we must use more detailed analyses in their social contexts of how people use language responding to influence others (see all the discursive analysis books and papers cited in Guerin, 2003, 2004, 2016a). And while 'perception = doing' for Gibson, he looked almost exclusively at 'moving' as the 'doing' part of perception. My argument has been that most of our doing-perception is language use (especially naming) and other social behaviours that are afforded when we look around us.

Assumption 4

We can use the language analyses and research from discourse analysis, sociolinguistics, and elsewhere to reconceptualize 'cognitive' phenomena in a much better contextual way (e.g. Edwards, 1997; Edwards & Potter, 1993; details are given later in Tables 8.1, 8.2, and 8.3). Like the analysis of verbal behaviour, these fields of research are also committed to studying *language use in its social context*, to show how people utilize language to do things to people (Guerin, 1997, 2003, 2016a). The common strategies and ways of talking and writing have already been explored in the social science fields and provide more sophisticated analyses than found in the early work by Skinner (1957), even though that was its aim.

Assumption 5

Following all the above, big inroads into exploding the theoretical 'cognitive' analyses can be made by considering that *thinking and consciousness are just language use but not out loud* (see Chapter 4). This places them as part of our 'normal' conversations and uses of language in our lives, with the only difference being that they are not said out loud. They are not 'talking to yourself' but talking in the absence of the normal audiences (that can occur for a variety of reasons as we saw in Chapter 4).

With this fifth assumption added, a huge array of ideas spring forth, and we can (potentially): observe thinking and consciousness; use discourse analysis to find out more about what thinking does in context; and replace a lot of the cognitive 'modules' that fill up cognitive theories and figures. As written elsewhere (Guerin, 2016b), if we know all about someone's life contexts (social relationships, economic, cultural, etc.), then we can potentially know what they will be thinking.

Thinking and consciousness are not therefore stuck inside our body or our heads. Thinking and consciousness become part of our lived, physical worlds, and our environments, plus our extensive language-use training, *afford* us thinking and consciousness. They do not usually appear to do so, they instead appear individual and hidden, because social contexts are difficult to see without a lot of effort and over time, and this leads people to want to stick with their dualisms and Pathway 1 approaches.

Assumption 6

Hence, to rethink most of the cognitive phenomena, especially what we commonly label as thinking and consciousness, we actually require a combination of anthropological methods and discourse analysis (Guerin, Leugi, & Thain, 2018).

Replacing some basic 'cognitive processes'

I have raised some problems above for cognitive theories (Guerin, 2016a) and given some assumptions to begin rethinking cognitive thinking. We find this difficult to change partly because Pathway 1 has permeated public media and everyday conversation. A salesperson asks a customer if they want to buy something and they reply: "Look, I am not sure. I have to go away and process this information more." Now this is probably a conversational strategy just to politely say "No", but the cognitive jargon is common, and so if you asked that person what they were going to do that night, they might answer: "Well, I will run the main pros and cons over in my head tonight, and then make a decision." But this is all theoretical modelling, and this certainly *does not constitute a description of what actually takes place as real events* that night (Ryle, 1971).

Some general changes to 'cognitive thinking'

To help rethink cognitive metaphors I will give some examples. I have written about some of these in books and papers but they have never been collected together, which is my aim here.

Table 8.1 gives some of these basic points of cognitive models as you might find them in a psychology textbook, and then presents a new version incorporating the assumptions that have just been outlined.

The word 'processing' is very abstract and means many different things to different people. In general, you should think of it as just meaning 'doing something', but it usually refers to how our *uses of language* affect other people. Remember from our assumptions that 'cognition' usually means the use of language, and so 'cognitive processing' just means *doing things with language*. (There are some uses of 'processing perceptual information' that need a different contextual analysis, see Chapter 5.)

Table 8.1 Main foundations of cognitive psychology theory and how they can be replaced with a contextual or discursive account

Cognitive approach	Contextual approach
People 'take in' information and then process	What we do, say, and think (all are variously called 'decisions') arise from the contexts in which we are embedded and that have shaped us in the past
The cognitive system computes to make decisions	The 'decisions' are 'made' (shaped by) in the contexts in which we live; we act within those contexts based on our past and the 'locus' for the decision-making is therefore external
The information 'taken in' is limited sometimes or is 'single channel' only	We can learn multiple verbal responses to situations but if 'rehearsing' as thoughts or saying out loud, then we can only speak one thing at a time
People 'take in' information, process it and then decide, for example, how to attribute causality to events and people	Instead we ask: "What effect does making that *causality attribution* have on people or has had on people in the past?" (Edwards & Potter, 1993)
People 'take in' information, process it, and that processing decides what beliefs they 'possess'	"What effect does telling people that belief have on people or has had on people in the past?"
People 'take in' information, process it and then make mistakes and have biases in what they decide	"What effect does telling people those 'biased' statements have on people or has had on people in the past?"
People do not do what they say they are going to do	Saying and doing both arise from social and other contexts but not necessarily the same ones; why would you expect them to always coincide?
'Metacognition': thinking or talking about your cognitive processes	What you do or say will be a part of your context, so it can give rise to other responding

How reframing verbally for people in therapy works to affect their other behaviour	Whatever a therapist says is part of a social context with a history of consequences, so the 'reframed thinking' does not control the future behaviour but behaviour can change from the social contexts of a therapist talking (indeed that is the idea)
We process information from local events around us through sensations and perceptions	Probably the strongest and most frequent thoughts that 'pop into our heads' resonate with our immediate contexts—the rest are 'quieter' conversations, unless of great consequence. So if you suddenly see someone steal another person's purse and run, most of your thinking will be conversations to tell now or later about this event as it unfolds. This thinking does not control your running and helping that person, but if you have had those behaviours shaped already you will likely do this
Dreaming shows the internal thoughts and cognitive processes because there is no external input	Things do not have to be present even when we are awake for social contexts to give rise to thoughts. I can be at work and suddenly a thought about my mother 'pops into my head'. Dreaming is no different except that many of the editing and critical thoughts (from different audiences) might not be present. This version also suggests two interesting properties: (1) *dreams appear weird* when we wake up because they are not connected to any of our immediate contexts upon waking (it's cold, need coffee, blankets askew, work today); and (2) since there is no context for them when you wake up, *you are unlikely to be able to say them*, so people report that they cannot remember (say) their dreams upon waking. This is because (usually) none of the people or surroundings that were in your dreams are present when you wake up … luckily!
People only use 10 per cent of their brain's cognitive capacity when they think	Forget what the brain does; what this means is that of all the external contexts and the consequences they afford, we attend to or speak only 10 per cent of those that are occurring

Note that we do not sit down and think about processing information. It just happens. What this means is that all our history of conversations and the situations we have in life bring all this about and we just behave or talk, so we need an analysis of those situations not of some 'processing architecture'.

Note also that sometimes we specially emphasize that we are going to sit down and 'consciously' process some information (usually important events in life), and spend effort doing this (like *Le Penseur*). But right there are the clues for analysing these special situations: some *social* situations lead us to develop conversations that might be said out loud later *justifying* what we think we are processing. Next time this happens to you, make some long and very honest observations about what is really happening here. You are having 'conversations' going on about what you might say to other people about the outcome, you are not actually 'processing' anything at all to 'decide' that outcome (in the cognitive sense).

Most of what was just said also applies to 'decision-making'. This is a dangerous term because it is so vague, and usually just means 'doing something' but again, it is normally 'cognitive' so it usually means 'doing something with language to people'. Whenever there is *any* change in our behaviour we can state, "Yes, I decided to do that", even though we really do not know what just happened or where that 'decision' came from (what in our worlds really led us to behave that way). Once again, any 'performance' of deep and meaningful decision-making (with lots of grimacing while you are 'deciding') is really about your social performance afterwards, and is not actually causing the decision-making (that is, behaviour change).

In this sense, decision-making is really about *negotiating the social impact* of the 'decision' with your major social audiences in life afterwards—getting conversational snippets ready to show off or to defend yourself. So, your 'internal' decision-making is more about developing conversations to socially negotiate with the people in your life about what you have done (but you do not develop them inside you either). It is not about the logic of what you end up doing, it is nothing like writing down the steps of a procedure and working through them as computers do.

Many cognitive theorists have appealed to two major 'motivations' in life (Guerin, 1997), or have suggested two systems or types of cognition and decision-making (e.g. Kahneman, Thalen, etc.). From our assumptions these clearly seem to delineate those behaviours not directly involving our uses of language to affect other people, and those behaviours that do.

All the behaviours in Table 8.2 under 'with language use' need to be analysed as uses of language and therefore will involve other people as the parts of the world we are changing with those behaviours. This needs to be remembered: if it involves language then it involves other people (see Chapter 3).

Table 8.2 Multiple terms for engaging with the world or engaging with the world through language and therefore other people

Without language use	With language use
Knowing how	Knowing that
System 1	System 2
Unconscious cognition	Conscious cognition
Mindlessness	Mindfulness
Wu wei (effortless action)	Yu wei (intentional action)
Tamed monkey mind	Untamed monkey mind
Automatic	Reflective
Implicit cognition	Explicit cognition
Direct contingency controlled	Verbal contingency controlled
Non-verbal behaviour	Verbal behaviour (including gestures)
Unconscious	Conscious
Unconscious system (Ucs)	Conscious/preconscious systems (Cs/Pcs)
Uncontrolled	Controlled
Associative	Deductive
Effortless	Effortful
Fast	Slow
Skilled	Rule-following

In a similar way to the above, two other common 'cognitive' constructs are about the uses humans make from the language system they learn, and therefore they also involve other people. 'Metacognition' involves social situations *where you think or talk about* your 'cognitive processes' (i.e. all of Table 8.1). These are social because the conversations and discourse snippets that occur in 'metacognition' are about describing stories to other people later on, and these stories can be made up or drawn from your history of similar conversations. You do not 'find' these metacognitive reports sitting inside your head as a screen dump of your mind.

Executive functioning from more recent cognitive theories is likewise about your uses of language that are built around our other behaviours, but we again have to remember that they are conversational reports *built for other people* not part of any behaviour change. Executive function research from cognitive psychology can, however, give us some interesting avenues for thought and research. Miyake et al. (2000) suggested three types of executive functioning (or three 'social situations'):

- *Inhibition*: refers to 'suppressing or resisting a prepotent (automatic) response'. That is, situations in which there is a normal way of behaving and the person 'uses their executive functioning' to *stop* that way of behaving. This is clearly important in therapies of many sorts. The different take on this here, however, is that the 'executive functioning' is actually coming from your social contexts and social audiences, and how you have conversations and arguments with them or try to justify your behaviours. It is not happening inside you and there is no 'you' running this inhibition show.

- *Set-shifting*: refers to situations in which you 'switch between task sets or response rules'. I instruct you to *not* get up when the bell rings (as you always do) and you have to start switching your 'sets' (your behaviours in other words). Once again, you can see that this is about social control either directly or through the conversations you need to have with me afterwards when it succeeds or not.

- *Working memory*: in the same way again, 'integrating new information with old information and maintaining it over time' really refers to being socially instructed to behave differently, and the word 'information' always suggests that we are *talking* about learning to talk differently and maintain this. For example: "Every time you see the word 'cognitive' I want you to say out loud, 'verbal'. See how long you can do that for."

So really, executive functioning is social shaping either over what you do or else over your later talking about what you did (or failed to do).

Uncertainty reduction, catharsis, cognitive dissonance, prototypes, and 'schema-driven thinking'

The following points are part of the hidden, underlying scaffolds that have been propping up cognitive theories without many people noticing. As a reaction to the old S–R behaviourisms with their reinforcers, drives, and needs, cognitive psychology imported two main 'drivers' of behaviour. These were refreshing in the 1960s but ultimately weak in their stated form. To help wean us off cognitive models, I will briefly give my 'social' versions of both these, which brings their social contexts back into play (see Guerin, 2001b).

The two main answers were (1) *uncertainty reduction* and (2) *catharsis* (dealt with more in what follows). Uncertainty reduction seeps through many cognitive models in different forms. The original Miller et al. (1960) version was that there was too much *information* (an elusive term; see V5.1) in the world for humans to take in and process, so humans *needed* to simplify the world and not deal with everything. In this way, we end up with schema, prototypes, dichotomies, etc. Our cognitive processing system is there supposedly to *take in* the world but *simplify* it so that we can easily remember and process what is important, and *not get overwhelmed*.

Sometimes this 'explanation' included a bit of catharsis as well (from Freud), that there was so much going on in our worlds that we might become stressed out and anxious, and this is why we have cognitive processing units—to simplify the world so we can deal with it better and avoid anxiety.

I have dealt with the flaws in this reasoning more closely elsewhere (Guerin, 2001b), so for now just notice how ad hoc this all is. Their arguments relied on William James's statement (with no evidence) that young babies are overwhelmed by the world and for them the world is a "blooming buzzing confusion". I have had four children and we never noticed this at all, however.

Jumping now to our assumptions mentioned earlier in the chapter, we can see that by 'simplifying the world' they really mean 'using language' instead of doing things in the world (see the perils of Chapter 7). And we *are* overwhelmed when we have to *tell someone* the complete details of what has happened, so we therefore have socially acceptable discourses that can replace giving all the gory details: "Yes, I felt a little sick yesterday so I took the day off", "All I saw in the park was a dog", "I see a triangle", are all we need to say. But this is only when we are *talking* about what is happening in our worlds and feel the need to justify, defend, or boast.

(To go back to Chapter 1 and the Gestalt triangle, when someone asks "What do you see?" socially it is not good to overwhelm (bore) them with a full description of the broken triangle and its lines and angles. "Too much information" we now say. So, unless our art professor asks the question as a trick, we just say (socially), "I see a triangle" and wait for a response on whether this was okay and what more was required.)

If we are *not talking* about what we are doing, then we can carry out amazingly complex and multitasking activities without being overwhelmed. If tennis stars, racing car drivers, video game players, runners, and others had to *talk about* what they were doing before doing it, or worse, during, then yes, it would be a blooming buzzing confusion. But we can do the complex activities and then have an acceptable way to simplify *in discourse* when we *tell* someone.

So, the uncertainty reduction drivers built into cognitive models are really about what we learn to do when we are *telling* other people about what we do, not when we are actually doing it (see Chapter 7 for some examples). The whole driver for cognitive models is therefore *social* and relevant only to *talking about* what we do (to be sure, that is very important in our lives). This is also one way how the 'social' was theoretically hidden away and ignored by importing the word 'information' for the cognitive revolution (V5.1).

Other cognitive theories followed *catharsis* more as their driver, foundation, or scaffold. We have already seen one version of this earlier in the chapter, that we supposedly get all anxious when there is too much information to take in, whereas I reframed that as: our situation is aversive when we have to *tell* someone about what we do or are going to do, especially if we think they will judge us.

Other cognitive theories proposed that *not knowing something is in itself aversive* and so we have a cognitive processing system to reduce what we do not know or to disguise it by simplifying. This is seen in a common but *wrong* explanation given for religion and elsewhere; we are supposedly anxious about not knowing the meaning of life or whether our existence has a purpose, so being religious reduces this anxiety. Freud used a similar form of explanation as well (Guerin, 2001b, V5.8).

Once again, with our contextual assumptions, we can see all these as *language uses* in a social context. Being uncertain or not knowing *is not* inherently anxiety provoking; I do not know what my dog is currently doing but that is not a big deal. However, being uncertain or not knowing *is* inherently anxiety provoking when this is in a social or language context. If my dog has gotten out several times and attacked some neighbours, then I *will* be anxious and wanting to do something about this (and be preparing what to say to my neighbours and the police if something bad has happened).

A common example in cognitive psychology of the discursive strategy of using catharsis is *cognitive dissonance*, which has also got into the popular media of late. This proposes that if we 'have' or 'believe' (these both need more analysis) contradictory thoughts 'in our head' then this produces an 'internal state' of dissonance or anxiety, and we therefore are 'driven' to reduce that state by changing one or more of these 'beliefs' (or by changing our behaviour sometimes). Some cognitive theories use this version of catharsis more specifically as the theoretical driver of behaviour.

In brief, contradictory thoughts are *not* a problem, just as we saw above that uncertainty and not knowing are not a problem (Guerin, 2001b). But once again, *having contradictory thoughts or beliefs is a problem when confronted with this socially, and this will occur through language use.*

I can tell my mother that I really like her new painting while at the same time I joke with my siblings later that her new painting is awful. This contradiction is not a problem and I will sleep ok at night. But, it *is* a problem when the two ways of talking get confronted: one of my siblings starts calling me two-faced behind my back; my mother finds out what I said to my siblings; I am telling my mother how lovely her new painting is in front of my siblings and I have to keep a straight face. In each case, the problem is that I have to get some discourse ready to deal with these new situations, but up until then, there was no anxiety about being contradictory.

What this is saying is that *cognitive dissonance is really social dissonance.* The classic cognitive dissonance experiments can be re-analysed in this way, since they had hidden social pressures in the experiments which were played down. Guerin (2001a) reanalysed some of these classic experiments in this way (also in V5.9).

In discussing thinking and concepts, cognitive psychology has been based on the idea that we process, remember, and recall 'information' not as complete and full data but as simplifications. We have already seen one misguided use of this logic. Two other versions of these you will come across are *schema-based thinking* and *prototypes*.

All that schema-based thinking and prototypes mean are, once again based on our assumptions listed earlier in the chapter, that we simplify *when using words* (remember our mantras: cognition equals language use and language use equals social behaviour). When we 'schematize' the world to simplify, this is only relevant to our use of language to deal with people. When we mow the lawns without talking (no stresses, social issues, or contradictions involved), then we have no need to 'schematize' mowing the lawns. We only need to schematize when we are *talking about* mowing the lawns: "Why didn't you do a proper job of mowing this time?" Mowing the lawns in itself requires no simplifications or schematizing (see Chapter 7).

Prototypes were proposed as another way to think about the simplification of our worlds (for talking, anyway). Instead of remembering and processing a 'dog' schema, or category, it was proposed that we remember and process a 'dog prototype'. This just means we base our simplification on a typical example or 'exemplar' (the word they often used). For a dog, this might be a Labrador, as a middle-of-the-road standard dog (sorry Labrador owners). We then 'process' all dogs in this way but with an indication of how different our actual dog is to the prototype dog that is stored away somewhere inside us: "I saw this lovely dog today in the park; it was sort of larger than your average dog and a strikingly different dark brown colour."

In a social context, prototypes can be viewed as a 'socially safe' way of talking that will not attract criticisms, mockery, etc. If you said to me, "Oh I saw a dog today", and I replied, "What? Like a chihuahua?", you would be puzzled since that is not a socially common dog to use as a reference (in fact, you would probably take it as a poor attempt at a joke).

So, all the cognitive psychology research on schema and prototypes can be seen as useful, but the theories are dubious. If we reframe this research instead as 'studying how people use language in ways that are *socially* fluent and acceptable', then there is useful material there. But we would need to look more closely at the social contexts in which people use these different language strategies and what happens when they do. This requires changing methodology from the typical cognitive psychology methodologies (as also per our Assumption 6), and so most of the cognitive psychology research would be lacking in this way (so far). An attempt to contextualize the common research practices is given elsewhere (V5.9).

Memory research, or 're-responding in context', needs to be handled in the same way to wean ourselves off cognitive models. Almost all the research on remembering is about verbal/social behaviour. Some 'perceptual remembering' (Kohler, Gibson) needs to be analysed in other ways (see Chapter 5).

So, when dealing with cognitive psychology and memory research we are dealing with discourse analysis, how people learn to talk and re-talk in certain ways in certain social contexts. For example, almost everything in cognitive psychology about remembering colours is about *speaking about colours*. But the same methodology problems as we have just mentioned exist here. For remembering, then, I will just leave you with one of my favourite quotes, which was written a long time before cognitive psychology even existed but needs to be resurrected:

> Memory, like belief, like all psychological phenomena, is an action; essentially, it is the action of telling a story. Almost always we are concerned here with a linguistic operation, quite independent of our attitude towards the happening. A sentinel outside the camp watches the coming of the enemy. When the enemy arrives, the first business of the sentinel is to perform particular actions related to this arrival; he must defend himself or must hide, must lie flat, crawl in order to escape notice, and make his way back to the camp. These are actions of adaptation demanded by the event, and the perception of an event is nothing else than the totality of such acts of adaption. But simultaneously with these acts of adaptation, the sentinel must exhibit a reaction of a new kind, a kind which is characteristic of memory; he must prepare a speech, must in accordance with certain conventions translate the event into words, so that he may be able ere long to tell history to the commander. This second reaction has important peculiarities which differentiate it markedly from the first reaction. The actions which comprised this, the action of self-defence, that of lying flat, that of hiding in one way or another, are no doubt preserved like all the tendencies; but they can only be reproduced, can only be activated anew, if the sentinel is again placed in the same circumstances, being faced by the same enemy and upon the same ground; they will not be reproduced in different circumstances, as for instance when the sentinel has gone back to camp, is among his comrades, and in the presence of his commander. On the other hand, the second reaction, his account of the matter, though it likewise is after a fashion adapted to the event, can readily be reproduced under new conditions when the sentinel is among his comrades in the presence of the commander, and when there is no sign of the enemy. The stimulus which will arouse the activation of this tendency is a special form of social action, a question. Thus the essential characteristic of the sentinel's story is that it is independent of the event to which it relates, whereas the reactions which comprise his perception have no such independence.

(Janet, 1919/1925, pp. 661–662)

Cognitive biases and heuristics

Labelling our human 'cognitive biases' has become very popular in the media and elsewhere thanks to people like Kahneman and Thaler. The basic phenomena seem robust, but it is the cognitive modelling and the explanations that I find shaky.

What has been learned is that humans do not make 'decisions' (this is socially negotiating the use of language, remember) on a totally rational consideration of outcomes. That much I do not dispute. But as the explanation of this, the cognitive models propose that our cognitive processing systems have limitations, faults, and inbuilt biases. So, this is a blame-the-victim explanation since our own faulty processing leads us into errors. I have a problem inside of me that make me do wrong things.

Going back to our assumptions, these biases are really about talking and discourses, language strategies we commonly use with people. My explanation instead is that when we *talk* about outcomes and 'decisions', such discourses *always include weighing or negotiating social outcomes as well*, and this is what 'leads us astray'; cf. V5.1). Remember? Language use is about negotiating social relationships, not the words themselves (see Chapter 3). With this alternative explanation, we do not blame the victim because taking account of social outcomes is extremely important in our lives and *we would be foolish not to take them into account*. Social context impacts on all our decisions, so we need to include this. Making decisions and not taking social outcomes into account is actually not rational, and probably does not exist outside of Western rationality ideas (V5.1).

In this way, the mathematicians and economists are the foolish ones because they work out decisions based on purely non-social outcomes and call those the best or optimal answers (V5.1). But as we all know from life, we can make whatever decisions we like but if we get the *social* outcomes wrong, all is lost anyway and what we propose will not work out.

In V5.1 I look at how Western ideas of 'rationality' have really meant 'excluding the social'. This is good for science and dealing with the non-social world, since we do not want our measurements of the wind-speed velocity of sparrows to be influenced by whom we happen to be talking to at the time. We do not want a science where $E = mC^2$ when talking to our mother but $E = 4mC^3$ when talking to our siblings. But I suggest that the application of this same 'rational' decision-making (which purposefully excludes the social, to mimic what science does successfully) to psychology, law, economics, mental health, government, bureaucracy, ecology, religion, and emotion, has been a big mistake (V5.1).

I hope it can be seen that acting 'irrationally' is always a case of strong alternative social consequences so it is not really irrational after all. To properly examine these 'decision biases', then, research should be looking at the hidden social outcomes for *saying* our answers to decision questions. This means that something like discourse analysis methods need to replace the primarily experimental, non-social methods used in all past research (like that by Kahneman, Tversky, and Thaler).

For example, if there is a choice between $10 and $20 in a typical experimental test of 'cognitive biases', I would be irrational to choose the $10, surely? However, a proper analysis of the outcomes must (rationally!) include any social outcomes of choosing $20. Such 'decisions' also depend on the *social contexts*, which are totally ignored (indeed, they are excluded from consideration as all context has been removed) in these experiments. It could be that if I took the $20 then people in my community or family would think I am greedy and I could lose many other useful social and economic consequences in the future because of doing that (if they found out, which would also be involved in *the real social context that has been excluded*). Which, then, is being irrational—ignoring the social effects and future social outcomes, or losing half the money? The experimental research only works with experimenters who are strangers (all very neoliberal!).

So, judgments of what are rational or 'irrational' choices actually require a more thorough knowledge of *all* the person's contexts, not just the one in focus currently, and especially of the social ones. For this reason, anthropologists and sociologists (e.g. Durkheim and Evans-Pritchard) have been very careful and wise to observe and analyse in great detail the *social context of so-called 'irrational behaviours'*. In fact, they make the point that there are no irrational behaviours, just ones that have different cultural and social contexts outcomes to ours. With their better contextual research methods, they have some of the best and most detailed examples of showing how 'irrational' behaviours turn out to be the most sophisticated, when seen in their total social, economic, and cultural context.

To put this boldly, if you wish to categorize behaviour as being *irrational* or as being *non-functional* (this is the DSM version of irrational; Guerin, 2017), this really means that you have not properly investigated all the contexts! And you cannot just say, 'Oh, those social reasons do not count', as doing *this* is irrational, actually.

Table 8.3 lists some of these 'cognitive biases' and particularly those used in clinical psychology to make judgements about people acting irrationally or 'dysfunctionally' (e.g. Beck, Rush, Shaw, & Emery, 1979). In the 'contextual or discourse analysis account' column I have added one *possible* discourse analysis of what might be going on; how the 'mistake' from the

Table 8.3 Several 'cognitive biases' from theories of cognitive psychology and clinical behavioural therapy, with an alternative contextual or discursive account

'Cognitive biases'	Common explanation or cognitive theory	Contextual or discourse analysis account
Anchoring	A cognitive bias wherein one relies too heavily on one trait or piece of information: "All I know is that she used the word 'jerk'"	People rely too heavily on what can be named (the 'information'), at the expense of what can be done but not named shaped by their contexts
Availability heuristic	When people predict the frequency of an event based on how easily an example can be brought to mind: "I can't see how she might possibly like me!"; "I can't think of anything or anyone that might help me"	Relying too heavily on what words can be said or thought ('come to mind') rather than their experience or wordless actions shaped by their contexts
Representativeness heuristic	Where people judge the probability or frequency of a hypothesis by considering how much the hypothesis resembles available data: "She used the word 'jerk' so she must hate me"	People follow words and the similarity between different verbal accounts (that arise from discursive experience and training) rather than on experience or non-word training shaped by their contexts
Optimistic bias (Guerin & Wood, 2017)	People claim they are better drivers than the average driver, and that bad events are less likely to happen to them than others	When people are asked these judgements (they probably do not even make them otherwise) they need to socially defend what they say. To do this they can only really compare what they (as an individual) can say about their own record and what they can say about the 'average' person's record, and this socially and verbally directed comparison leads to overestimation of own luck
Arbitrary inference	Jumping to a conclusion without good reason: Might be mind-reading, "I know she is going to reject me", or assuming the outcomes, "It's not even worth going because I know I am going to fail"	Reason giving and establishing (wrong) facts that are convincing Use of extremes are common Making presumptions that are probably incorrect but difficult to notice in conversation Strategizing statements to make them look 'as if' they are facts

(*continued*)

Table 8.3 Cont.

'Cognitive biases'	Common explanation or cognitive theory	Contextual or discourse analysis account
Selective abstraction	Focusing on one aspect of a situation and ignoring the rest: "I will fail because I made one mistake right in the middle"	Use of partial facts Making presumptions that are probably incorrect but difficult to notice in conversation Using categories incorrectly as a strategy
Overgeneralization	Overstating that if something happened once it will always happen: "I don't like going to parties. I tried it once and it was awful"	Use of extremes Use of abstraction to make challenging more difficult
Magnification and minimization	Minimizing positive outcomes and maximizing negative outcomes: exaggerating or catastrophizing	Use of extremes or hedges to maximize and minimize
Personalization	Falsely taking responsibility for something bad: "My child failed their test. I am such a bad parent." Blaming: Doing the same but putting the responsibility onto someone else entirely	Discursive placement of responsibility in the opposite way to usual strategies (you are responsible for good outcomes, other people for bad outcomes) Question to analyse is: what are the other contextual arrangements so this is arrived at?
Dichotomous thinking	Thinking in black and white; you are either a good or a bad person	Strategic use of word categories to establish facts
Ignoring the positive or filtering	Focus on the negative aspects only: "The boss said I did well in the interview but he gave me one strange look in the middle that I think said it all!" Disqualifying or discounting the positive is similar: "She said she liked me but I know she only felt she had to say that"	Reason giving in reverse of the usual pattern (emphasizing the negative rather than positive because of the particular social context)

'bias' really results from the way we socially use language in everyday life, and how that social context is ignored in experimental research and clinical settings.

To spell out just one example, the 'anchoring bias' of Kahneman and Tversky shows that people rely too heavily on certain traits (note how verbal this is!) or 'pieces of information' and this leads their decisions astray (see Chapter 7). From a contextual, behaviour analytic, or ecological framework, on the other hand, this shows that *people rely in conversation too much on what can be named* (because that allows you to report it or make a story about it) and the multitasking nuances of real life get lost—all the nuances are probably not lost when carrying out the behaviours, but *are lost when talking about your behaviours*. These are the 'gaps' mentioned in Chapter 7.

References

Beck, A. T., Rush, A., Shaw, B. F., & Emery, G. (1979). *Cognitive therapy of depression*. New York, NY: Guilford Press.

Edwards, D. (1997). *Discourse and cognition*. London: Sage.

Edwards, D., & Potter, J. (1993). Language and causation: A discursive action model of description and attribution. *Psychological Review, 100*, 23–41.

Gibson, J. J. (1950). *The perception of the visual world*. Boston, MA: Houghton Mifflin.

Gibson, J. J. (1960). The concept of the stimulus in psychology. *American Psychologist, 15*, 694–703.

Gibson, J. J. (1966). *The senses considered as perceptual systems*. Boston, MA: Houghton Mifflin.

Gibson, J. J., & Gibson, E J. (1955). Perceptual learning: Differentiation or enrichment? *Psychological Review, 62*, 32–41.

Guerin, B. (1997). How things get done: Socially, non-socially; with words, without words. In L. J. Hayes & P. Ghezzi (Eds.), *Investigations in behavioral epistemology* (pp. 219–235). Reno, NV: Context Press.

Guerin, B. (2001a). Individuals as social relationships: 18 ways that acting alone can be thought of as social behavior. *Review of General Psychology, 5*, 406–428.

Guerin, B. (2001b). Replacing catharsis and uncertainty reduction theories with descriptions of the historical and social context. *Review of General Psychology, 5*, 44–61.

Guerin, B. (2003). Language use as social strategy: A review and an analytic framework for the social sciences. *Review of General Psychology, 7*, 251–298.

Guerin, B. (2004). *Handbook for analyzing the social strategies of everyday life*. Reno, NV: Context Press.

Guerin, B. (2016a). *How to rethink human behavior: A practical guide to social contextual analysis*. London: Routledge.

Guerin, B. (2016b). *How to rethink psychology: New metaphors for understanding people and their behavior*. London: Routledge.

Guerin, B. (2017). *How to rethink mental illness: The human contexts behind the labels.* London: Routledge.

Guerin, B., Leugi, G. B., & Thain, A. (2018). Attempting to overcome problems shared by both qualitative and quantitative methodologies: Two hybrid procedures to encourage diverse research. *Australian Community Psychologist, 29,* 74–90.

Guerin, B., & Wood, E. (2017). Why do adolescents lie in the sun when they know it is risky? Contextualizing the 'attitude–behavior' gap and the 'optimistic bias' as verbal behaviour. *Educere et Educare: Revista de Educação, 13,* 1–15.

Janet, P. (1919/1925). *Psychological healing: A historical and clinical study.* London: George Allen & Unwin.

Miller, G. A., Galanter, E., & Pribram, K. H. (1960). *Plans and the structure of behavior.* New York, NY: Holt, Rinehart & Winston.

Miyake, A., Friedman, N. P., Emerson, M. J., Witzki, A. H., Howerter, A., & Wager, T. D. (2000). The unity and diversity of executive functions and their contributions to complex 'frontal lobe' tasks: A latent variable analysis. *Cognitive Psychology, 41,* 49–100.

Prior, A. (1960). The run-about inference ticket. *Analysis, 21,* 38–39.

Ryle, G. (1971). The thinking of thoughts: What is 'Le Penseur' doing? In G. Ryle, *Collected papers. Volume 2: Collected essays 1929–1968* (pp. 480–496). London: Hutchinson.

Skinner, B. F. (1935). The generic nature of the concepts of stimulus and response. *Journal of General Psychology, 12,* 40–65.

Skinner, B. F. (1957). *Verbal behavior.* Englewood Cliffs, NJ: Prentice Hall.

Index

Note: Page numbers in **bold** refer to tables and in *italics* to figures.